Bottomless BRUNCH

A DAZZLING COLLECTION OF
BRUNCH RECIPES PAIRED WITH
THE PERFECT COCKTAIL

Bottomless
BRUNCH

A DAZZLING COLLECTION OF
BRUNCH RECIPES PAIRED WITH
PERFECT COCKTAILS

WITH PHOTOGRAPHY BY KATE WHITAKER

RYLAND PETERS & SMALL
LONDON • NEW YORK

Designer Paul Tilby
Creative Director Leslie Harrington
Editorial Director Julia Charles
Production Manager
  Gordana Simakovic
Indexer Hilary Bird

First published in 2023 by
Ryland Peters & Small
20–21 Jockey's Fields
London WC1R 4BW
and
341 E 116th St, New York NY 10029

www.rylandpeters.com

10 9 8 7 6 5 4 3 2 1

Recipe collection compiled by
Julia Charles. Introduction by
Alice Sambrook © Ryland Peters
& Small 2023.

Text copyright © Val Aikman-Smith,
Julia Charles, Liz Franklin, Laura
Gladwin, Tori Haschka, Carol Hilker,
Vicky Jones, Kathy Kordalis, Uyen
Luu, Theo A. Michaels, Hannah Miles,
Louise Pickford & Shelagh Ryan.

Design and photographs copyright
© Ryland Peters & Small 2023

UK ISBN: 978-1-78879-575-3
US ISBN: 978-1-78879-524-1

Printed in China

A CIP record for this book is available
from the British Library.

US Library of Congress Cataloguing-
in-Publication Data has been applied
for.

NOTES
• Ryland Peters & Small do not
advocate overconsumption or the
abuse of alcohol. While we hope you
will try the recipes and ideas in this
book, we hope you will do so with
responsibility.

• Both British (Metric) and American
(Imperial oz. plus US cups) are
included in these recipes for your
convenience, however it is important
to work with one set of measurements
and not alternate between the two
within a recipe.

• All spoon measurements are
level, unless otherwise specified.
A tablespoon is 15 ml and a teaspoon
is 5 ml.

• When a recipe calls for the grated
zest of citrus fruit, buy unwaxed fruit
and wash well before using. If you
can only find treated fruit, scrub well
in warm soapy water before using.

FSC
www.fsc.org
MIX
Paper | Supporting
responsible forestry
FSC® C008047

CONTENTS

INTRODUCTION

Ahh bottomless brunching, the most decadent of pastimes. Picture the scene: there's no work today so you wake up a little later than normal, feeling refreshed from those extra minutes snoozing. You roll out of bed and take your time getting ready, looking forward to meeting up with friends or loved ones. Tummy rumbling slightly, you're already fantasising about the delicious food and drink that are coming your way for a late breakfast/early lunch. Maybe you're celebrating something exciting like a birthday or hen/bachelorette party, or maybe just rejoicing in having made it through a long working week. Either way, what could be more pleasant than a fancy brunch paired with as much of your choice beverage as you could possibly desire? It's the perfect way to celebrate like a rockstar and be chilling in your PJs come evening (a.k.a., the dream).

With this book, you can invite everyone over and enjoy the glorious concept of bottomless brunching in the comfort of your own kitchen. The benefits? You get to pick the recipes to create your perfect menu *and* it's less expensive than going out… plus you can take yourself off for a little nap whenever you please. Because if you are opting for booze, bottomless brunches are often best undertaken with the caution of having little to no plans for later. When the mimosas start flowing by midday, you'll wish you didn't have that afternoon Pilates class or tea with grandparents booked in…

Of course, not everyone wants to be dancing on tables by 3pm, so as well as classic cocktails, this book offers a whole host of interesting low- and no-alcohol drinking options to complement your cuisine.

From dainty, sweet brunches to savoury meals that really line the stomach, there is something to suit all tastes and every occasion. Try a sophisticated lighter bite in the **Californian** chapter, such as the Superfood Bowls with Smoked Salmon, Quinoa and Avocado, washed down with Green Piña Colada Smoothies. Sample a classy brunch dish from the **Italian** section, like the Caprese Skillet eggs with Aperol Spritz for afters. You could opt for a gorgeous pastry from the **Parisian** pages, such as Pretzel Croissants paired with Kir Royales. Or how about a filling **Tex-Mex** dish like Steak and Egg Tacos with as many Jalapeño Margaritas as you can muster? There's a **Levantine** inspired chapter with mouth-watering dishes like Socca Pancakes with Charred Asparagus and Labneh, which you can enjoy with refreshing Pomegranate and Mint Green Tea. If you've got a hearty appetite, then attempt the Oyster Rockefeller Hash from the **American** section alongside

Cool and Dirty Martinis. Peruse the **Asian-style** chapter for delights such as Spicy Pork Burgers with Mango Salsa, perhaps served with Lime, Cucumber and Lychee Gin and Tonics. Take inspiration from the sunny **Mediterranean** section and try the Rosti with Green Tomato Soffritto paired with Apricot and Basil Mimosas. Finally, you could comfort yourself with a warming brunch from the **Winter Comforts** section such as fluffy Poppyseed Pancakes with Crushed Cinnamon Raspberries and a pitcher of Fireside Sangria.

Forget late night dinner parties, host a bottomless brunch for friends at home and you'll have the whole day of fun ahead of you. There's a reason why this trend has stuck around: the bottomless brunching mindset is one of pure relaxation; no time constraints, commute or stress… just scrumptious food and bountiful drink for limitless enjoyment.

CALIFORNIAN

STRAWBERRY, BANANA & ALMOND SMOOTHIE BOWL

THIS DISH LOOKS SO PRETTY WITH ALL OF ITS ADORNMENTS. FEEL FREE TO SUBSTITUTE DIFFERENT FRUITS, NUT BUTTERS AND TOPPINGS THAT YOU HAVE TO HAND. TO GET AHEAD, FREEZE SMALL BAGS WITH THE BANANA, STRAWBERRIES AND OATS READY TO WHIZZ UP WITH THE MILK, YOGURT AND NUT BUTTER BEFORE ADDING YOUR TOPPINGS. THIS SMOOTHIE BOWL FOR ONE IS REALLY EASY TO SCALE UP IF FEEDING A CROWD.

200 g/1 cup strawberries, frozen
1 banana, peeled and frozen
60 g/generous ½ cup jumbo rolled oats
125 ml/½ cup almond milk
120 g/½ cup Greek yogurt (or coconut yogurt for a vegan version)
30 g/2 tablespoons almond butter (or any nut butter)
10 g/2 teaspoons clear honey (or maple syrup for a vegan version)

TO SERVE
blueberries, sliced banana, toasted muesli, goji berries and/or chia seeds

SERVES 1

Place all the smoothie ingredients into a blender and blitz until smooth and creamy.

Pour into a shallow breakfast bowl and decorate as shown with blueberries, sliced banana, toasted muesli, goji berries and/or chia seeds. Serve at once.

FISHERMAN'S WHARF BENEDICT ON SOURDOUGH

THIS TAKE ON THE CLASSIC EGGS BENEDICT IS AN ODE TO SAN FRANCISCO'S FAMED FISHERMAN'S WHARF, WHERE ONE CAN GRAB A CRAB SANDWICH AND EAT IT AMONGST A BACKDROP OF SEAGULLS AND SEA AIR. THIS RECIPE ALSO USES CHÈVRE CHEESE AND AVOCADO – TWO OTHER THINGS CALIFORNIA DOES SO WELL!

4 slices of sourdough bread
450 g/3 cups shredded/picked
   over good-quality crab meat,
   at room temperature
8 eggs
120 g/4 oz. chèvre goat's cheese,
   sliced into quarters
2 ripe avocados, halved, stoned/
   pitted and sliced

LEMON HOLLANDAISE
6 egg yolks
finely grated zest of 1 small lemon
2 tablespoons Dijon mustard
340 g/1½ cups unsalted butter,
   melted
½ teaspoon salt
⅛ teaspoon freshly ground black
   pepper
⅛ teaspoon paprika

a double boiler (optional)

SERVES 4

Start by making the lemon hollandaise. In a small saucepan or pot set over a low heat, bring 5 cm/2 inches of water to a bare simmer. Place a metal bowl over the pot to form a bain-marie (or use a double boiler, if you have one).

Add the yolks, lemon zest and mustard to the bowl of the bain-marie and whisk constantly until the mixture is thickened and ribbons form when you pull this whisk away from the bowl (this should take about 4–5 minutes). The yolks should double or triple in volume.

Slowly whisk in the melted butter, stirring constantly. Once the butter is fully incorporated, add the salt, pepper and paprika and continue whisking for about 3 minutes, until thick. If the mixture is too thick, add a little hot water as needed. Adjust the seasoning to taste. Remove from the heat and set aside.

Preheat the oven to 230°C (450°F) Gas 8.

Cut the sourdough bread in half and arrange on a baking sheet in a single layer. Bake until toasted, about 5 minutes. Put two sourdough halves on each plate and top with crab, dividing evenly.

To poach the eggs, bring 2.5 cm/1 inch water to the boil in a medium pan. Lower the heat so that small bubbles form on the bottom of the pan and break to the surface only occasionally.

Crack the eggs into the water one at a time, holding the shells close to the water's surface and letting the eggs slide out gently. Poach the eggs, in two batches to keep them from crowding, 6 minutes for soft-cooked. Lift the eggs out with a slotted spoon, pat dry with a paper towel, and place one egg on each crab-topped sourdough half.

Top each egg with 2–3 tablespoons of the lemon hollandaise (gently reheated if necessary), and top with the goat's cheese and sliced avocado. Serve at once.

BEETROOT PANCAKES WITH GOAT'S CHEESE, ONION RELISH & WALNUTS

THE BEETROOT/BEET ADDS ATTRACTIVE COLOUR TO THESE SAVOURY PANCAKES, AS WELL AS A HINT OF EARTHY FLAVOUR. A LITTLE RYE FLOUR IS USED IN THE BATTER HERE TOO FOR ITS DEEP, STRONG TASTE, BUT IT CAN BE EASILY REPLACED WITH PLAIN/ALL-PURPOSE FLOUR.

2 eggs
220 ml/scant 1 cup whole milk
75 g/½ cup plus 1 tablespoon plain/all-purpose flour
25 g/3 tablespoons rye flour
a pinch of salt
55 g/2 oz. cooked beetroot/beet, finely chopped
1 tablespoon olive oil, plus extra for frying
rocket/arugula, fresh basil leaves and Parmesan shavings, to serve

FILLING
300 g/10½ oz. frozen spinach, thawed
300 g/10½ oz. soft goat's cheese
2 tablespoons freshly chopped basil
50 g/⅓ cup chopped walnuts
6 tablespoons grated Parmesan cheese

ONION RELISH
2 tablespoons olive oil
3 onions, thinly sliced
2 tablespoons balsamic vinegar
2 tablespoons soft brown sugar
sea salt and freshly ground black pepper

MAKES 16 PANCAKES

Start by making the onion relish. Heat the olive oil in a saucepan over a low-medium heat. Add the onions and a little salt and pepper and cook for 20 minutes, stirring occasionally, until they are really soft and golden. Add the vinegar and sugar and cook for a further 5–10 minutes until jammy in consistency. Leave to cool.

To make the pancakes, place the eggs, half the milk, the flours, salt and chopped beetroot/beet in a food processor and blend until the beetroot/beet is puréed and the mixture is smooth. Add the remaining milk and the oil and blend again. Transfer to a jug/pitcher and leave to rest for 20 minutes.

Meanwhile, make the filling. Squeeze out all the excess water from the thawed spinach and chop finely. Place in a bowl and beat in the goat's cheese, basil, walnuts and grated Parmesan. Season to taste with salt and pepper.

Lightly stir the pancake mixture once. Heat a frying pan/skillet over a medium heat, brush with oil and swirl in about 60 ml/¼ cup of the pancake mixture, making sure it covers the base. Cook over a medium-low heat for about 1½ minutes until the base is golden. Flip the pancake over and cook for a further 1 minute until dotted brown. Remove the pancake from the pan as soon as it is ready and keep warm while you cook the remaining batter in the same way.

When you are ready to serve, spoon the goat's cheese mixture down the centre of each pancake. Top with a few rocket/arugula leaves, fresh basil leaves and a spoonful of the onion relish. Roll up and enjoy. Serve the pancakes with extra relish and shavings of Parmesan cheese.

Serve with *Green Piña Colada Smoothie*, recipe on page 24

SUPERFOOD BOWL WITH SMOKED SALMON, QUINOA & AVOCADO

YOU CAN MAKE THIS BOWL VEGETARIAN BY USING GRILLED HALLOUMI INSTEAD OF THE SMOKED SALMON, AND VEGAN IF YOU OMIT IT ALTOGETHER. IT IS ALSO GLUTEN-FREE. REMEMBER TO ALLOW TIME TO SOAK THE CASHEW NUTS FOR THE DRESSING.

300 g/10½ oz. curly kale

2 teaspoons tamari

2 teaspoons apple cider vinegar

4 tablespoons plus 2 teaspoons olive oil

200 g/1 cup quinoa

1 head of broccoli (approx. 350 g/12 oz.), cut into long bite-sized florets

seeds from ½ pomegranate

1 long red chilli/chile, deseeded and thinly sliced

15 g/½ oz. dill, roughly chopped

grated zest of ½ lemon

2 tablespoons freshly squeezed lemon juice

2 ripe avocados

200 g/1 cup sliced smoked salmon

15 g/2 tablespoons pumpkin seeds/pepitas, toasted

sea salt and freshly ground black pepper

CASHEW TURMERIC YOGURT DRESSING

140 g/1 generous cup raw unsalted cashew nuts

1 tablespoon maple syrup

300 g/1½ cups Greek yogurt

1 teaspoon apple cider vinegar

½ teaspoon sea salt

1 teaspoon ground turmeric

1 teaspoon olive oil

SERVES 4

To make the cashew dressing, put the cashew nuts in a small bowl and cover with water. Allow the nuts to soak in room-temperature water for a couple of hours, or overnight. Drain the cashews and blitz in a blender with the other ingredients. The dressing will keep in the fridge in a sealed container for up to 1 week and is delicious with any salad or vegetables.

To make the salad, pull the kale from its central stalks and tear the leaves into small pieces. Put the kale in a bowl and add the tamari, apple cider vinegar and 2 teaspoons of olive oil. Scrunch it in your hands for a minute to coat the leaves and soften them a little.

Rinse the quinoa and place in a saucepan with double the volume of salted water and bring to the boil. Reduce the heat and simmer gently for 12 minutes until cooked. Drain into a colander and cool.

Bring a separate saucepan of salted water to the boil. Add the broccoli florets and simmer for a couple of minutes, then drain and run under cold water so the broccoli stays crunchy and does not continue to cook.

In a large bowl, combine the cooked quinoa, kale, broccoli, pomegranate seeds, chilli/chile and dill.

Make a lemon dressing by putting the lemon zest, lemon juice, 4 tablespoons olive oil and salt and pepper in a small screw-top jar. Shake, then pour over the quinoa salad mix and toss together.

Cut the avocados in half, stone/pit, then remove the flesh and slice. Distribute the quinoa salad between four bowls. Arrange the avocado and smoked salmon slices over the top of the salad in each bowl, then drizzle with the Cashew Turmeric Yogurt Dressing. Finally, sprinkle with the toasted pumpkin seeds/pepitas and serve.

Serve with Flavoured Waters, recipes on page 25

SMASHED AVOCADO ON TOAST WITH COURGETTE & HERB SALAD & DUKKAH

AVOCADOS CONTINUE TO REIGN SUPREME IN THE WORLD OF BRUNCH. THE NUTTY DUKKAH ADDS GREAT TEXTURE AND SALTINESS TO COUNTERBALANCE THE CREAMINESS OF THE AVOCADO AND THE COURGETTE/ZUCCHINI SALAD GIVES IT A WONDERFUL FRESHNESS.

2 ripe avocados
1 tablespoon freshly squeezed
 lemon juice
1 small courgette/zucchini
 (approx. 100 g/3½ oz.)
15 g/½ oz. mixed fresh herb
 leaves, such as mint, coriander/
 cilantro and flat-leaf parsley
2 teaspoons extra virgin olive oil
1 teaspoon grated lemon zest

2 slices of sourdough bread,
 toasted
2 tablespoons Dukkah (see below)
sea salt and freshly ground
 black pepper

DUKKAH
100 g/1 cup whole hazelnuts
20 g/¼ cup pistachio nuts
2 tablespoons coriander seeds
1 tablespoon cumin seeds

5 tablespoons sesame seeds
2 teaspoons white or black
 peppercorns
½ teaspoon dried chilli/hot red
 pepper flakes
½ teaspoon sea salt

a pestle and mortar

SERVES 2

First, make the dukkah. Preheat the oven to 160°C (324°F) Gas 3. Place the hazelnuts and pistachio nuts on separate small baking sheets and roast in the preheated oven for 10 minutes. Remove from the oven and immediately wrap the hazelnuts in a clean kitchen towel. Set aside to allow the steam to build for a minute before rubbing them within the kitchen towel to remove the loose skins. When both the pistachio nuts and hazelnuts are cool, roughly crush them using a pestle and mortar to a chunky texture. Transfer the mixture to a large mixing bowl.

Place the coriander and cumin seeds in a preheated dry frying pan/skillet set over a medium heat. Dry-fry the seeds for a couple of minutes, shaking the pan from time to time, until they start to pop. Remove the seeds from the pan and crush using the pestle and mortar. Add to the nuts in the mixing bowl.

Place the sesame seeds in the same dry pan and toast until lightly golden, giving the pan a shake every 30 seconds. Remove from the pan and grind using the pestle and mortar. Add to the nut and seed mixture. Repeat this process with the peppercorns.

Lightly grind the chilli/hot red pepper flakes using the pestle and mortar and add to the nut and seed mixture. Finally, add the salt and mix everything together to combine.

Cut the avocados in half, remove the stones/pits and scoop out the flesh into a bowl. Roughly mash the flesh with a fork, keeping it quite chunky. Add the lemon juice with a generous pinch of sea salt and black pepper. Gently combine.

To make the courgette/zucchini salad, use a mandolin or vegetable peeler to slice the courgette/zucchini into long thin ribbons. Place into a bowl with the herb leaves, olive oil, lemon zest and a pinch of salt and pepper. Toss together.

Spread the smashed avocado generously onto the two slices of sourdough toast. Heap the courgette/zucchini salad on top and sprinkle with the dukkah.

Note: Any leftover dukkah can be stored in an airtight container for up to 2 weeks.

Serve with Best Ever Bloody Mary, recipe on page 26

SEEDED BAKED PANCAKE WITH BERRIES & COCOA SAUCE

BASED ON A DUTCH PANCAKE THAT IS BAKED IN THE OVEN, THIS IS A SUPER-EASY AND DELICIOUS WAY TO MAKE A PANCAKE TO SERVE STRAIGHT FROM THE PAN. THIS ONE IS PACKED FULL OF NUTRITIOUS SEEDS AND SERVED WITH BERRIES AND A HEALTHY-ISH COCOA SAUCE FOR A TRULY POWER-PACKED BRUNCH.

PANCAKE BATTER
50 g/generous ⅓ cup plain/
　all-purpose flour
3 tablespoons coconut flour
1 teaspoon baking powder
a pinch of salt
150 ml/⅔ cup milk
3 eggs, beaten
4 tablespoons runny honey
1 teaspoon vanilla extract
5 tablespoons mixed seeds, such
　as linseeds/flaxseeds, chia
　seeds, sunflower seeds,
　poppy seeds
2 tablespoons coconut oil

COCOA SAUCE
4 tablespoons raw cocoa powder
2½ tablespoons runny honey
2½ tablespoons coconut oil,
　melted

TO SERVE
150 g/¾ cup Greek yogurt
50 g/1¾ oz. dried berries, such as
　goji, acai, cranberries etc.
100 g/3½ oz. mixed fresh berries
　such as blueberries, raspberries,
　redcurrants etc.
icing/confectioners' sugar, to dust

*23-cm/9-inch ovenproof frying pan/
　skillet*

SERVES 4

Preheat the oven to 200°C (400°F) Gas 6.

To make the pancakes, sift the plain/all-purpose flour, coconut flour, baking powder and salt into a mixing bowl. Combine the milk, eggs, honey and vanilla in a separate bowl and beat into the flours to make a smooth batter. Fold in the mixed seeds.

Heat the coconut oil in the ovenproof frying pan/skillet until melted. Pour in the pancake batter and transfer to the preheated oven. Bake in the preheated oven for 15 minutes until the pancake is puffed up and golden.

Meanwhile, make the cocoa sauce. Place all the ingredients in a saucepan with 4 tablespoons water and heat gently, stirring, until smooth. Keep warm.

As soon as the pancake is cooked, remove it from the oven. Spoon the yogurt into the centre and top with the dried and fresh berries. Drizzle over the cocoa sauce and serve at once, dusted with a little icing/confectioners' sugar.

Green Piña Colada Smoothie

Tropical goodness in a glass – or why not add a shot of Malibu to make it just a little bit naughty!

1 pineapple, peeled, cored and
    roughly chopped
1 banana
juice of 1 lime
100 ml/scant ½ cup coconut milk
180 ml/¾ cup Malibu coconut-
    flavoured white rum (optional)
a large handful of spinach
ice cubes

SERVES 6

Add all the ingredients to a blender and blitz together for a smooth consistency. Add Malibu for a dirty one. Pour into six tall glasses and serve at once.

NOTE ON ICE CUBES

Freeze edible flowers by working in layers. Fill an ice tray half full with water, add flowers facing down, and freeze. Add more water to the top and freeze. Use the same method for citrus fruits. Have fun with these – cut them into rounds or wedges (a wedge is perfect for a G & T). They are used in the Flavoured Waters, pictured on the facing page.

Flavoured Waters

Be creative and come up with exciting variations of flavoured water. The addition of iced edible flowers brings an ethereal touch (see page 24).

LEMONGRASS & CUCUMBER
2 lemongrass stalks, bruised
1 small cucumber, thinly pared
ice cubes
1.5 litres/6 cups water (or enough to fill the jug/pitcher)

SERVES 6

Mix the lemongrass, cucumber, ice and water in a large jug/pitcher and serve.

CITRUS
½ grapefruit, thinly sliced
1 lemon, thinly sliced
ice cubes
1.5 litres/6 cups water (or enough to fill the jug/pitcher)

SERVES 6

Mix the citrus fruit, ice and water in a large jug/pitcher and serve.

STRAWBERRY & BASIL
5 strawberries, hulled and quartered
a bunch of fresh basil
ice cubes
1.5 litres/6 cups water (or enough to fill the jug/pitcher)

SERVES 6

Mix the hulled strawberries, basil, ice and water in a large jug/pitcher and serve.

Best Ever Bloody Mary

A Bloody Mary is the ultimate brunch drink, allowing you to ingest booze before midday with complete legitimacy and even a hint of old-fashioned sophistication. Roast tomatoes add a deep and rich flavour, but you can substitute these for fresh tomatoes if you're short of time.

400 g/2½ cups cherry vine tomatoes
olive oil, for drizzling
500 ml/2 cups tomato juice
2 tablespoons Worcestershire sauce
2 tablespoons sriracha chilli/chili sauce
a 3-cm/1¼-inch piece of fresh horseradish, peeled and finely grated
60 ml/¼ cup freshly squeezed lime juice
300 ml/1¼ cups vodka
sea salt and freshly ground black pepper

TO GARNISH
celery stalks
chilli/hot red pepper flakes

SERVES 4

Preheat the oven to 180°C (350°F) Gas 4. Place the tomatoes on a baking sheet, drizzle with olive oil and season with salt and pepper. Roast for 15–20 minutes, or until the skins begin to split.

Put the tomato juice and roast tomatoes in a food processor and blend until smooth. Transfer to a large jug/pitcher and stir in the Worcestershire sauce, sriracha chilli/chili sauce and grated horseradish. Season with salt and pepper, cover with clingfilm/plastic wrap and chill in the fridge for at least 30 minutes.

When ready to serve, add the lime juice and vodka and stir well. Place a celery stalk in four highball glasses, half-fill each glass with ice and pour in the Bloody Mary mixture. Garnish each with a pinch of chilli/hot red pepper flakes and enjoy!

ITALIAN

FRESH SPINACH & HERB FRITTATE

THESE VENETIAN-STYLE SAUCER-SIZED FRITTATE ARE A PERFECT BRUNCH DISH. YOU
COULD MAKE THEM IN A NON-STICK MINI WOK ON THE STOVE OR IN VERY SMALL,
LIGHTLY OILED CAKE PANS, OR EVEN MAKE ONE LARGE FRITTATA AND CUT IT INTO
SQUARES OR TRIANGLES. YOU CAN VARY THE VEGGIES AND EVEN ADD GRATED CHEESE.

a large handful of fresh spinach
4–5 tablespoons extra virgin
   olive oil
1 small onion, finely chopped
6 eggs, beaten
a handful of mixed fresh herbs
   (such as flat-leaf parsley, basil
   and chives), finely chopped
salt and freshly ground black
   pepper

MAKES 3 MINI FRITTATE

Wash the spinach thoroughly and squeeze lightly to remove excess
water. Cook the spinach in a small saucepan over a medium heat until
it is wilted – this should only take 2–3 minutes. Set aside to cool, then
chop well and place in a bowl.

Heat 2 tablespoons of the oil in a small frying pan/skillet and cook the
onion until it is soft but still translucent. Leave it to cool a little, then
add it to the spinach and mix well. Add the beaten eggs and mix well.
Season to taste with salt and pepper, then stir in the chopped herbs.

Add a little of the remaining oil to a very small omelette/omelet pan or
mini wok set over a medium heat and pour in one-third of the mixture.
Using a non-stick spoon or spatula, draw the egg mixture from the
sides of the pan into the middle, until the whole frittata begins to set.
Turn the heat down to low and let the frittata continue to cook until
completely set (if you wish, flip it over at this stage). When fully set,
remove the pan from the heat and keep warm. Repeat with the
remaining mixture.

If preferred, you could preheat the oven to 180°C (350°F) Gas 4 and
divide the mixture between three small saucer-size cake pans, and cook
for about 20 minutes, until set. Or alternatively pour the whole lot into
a roasting pan and cook for about 30 minutes.

Cut into slices or squares and serve warm.

CAPRESE SKILLET

THIS SATISFYING SKILLET BRUNCH IS A GREAT COMBINATION OF A CLASSIC ITALIAN INSALATA CAPRESE (A SUBLIME COMBINATION OF MOZZARELLA, TOMATO AND FRESH BASIL) AND EGGS. THE TOMATOES WILL BE A LITTLE LIQUEFIED, BUT THE BREAD IS THERE TO SOAK UP ALL THOSE DELICIOUS JUICES! DRIZZLE WITH A GOOD AGED BALSAMIC VINEGAR FOR EXTRA ZING.

2 tablespoons olive oil
½ white onion, finely chopped
3 tomatoes, thinly sliced
½ teaspoon salt
½ teaspoon ground black pepper
4 eggs
200 g/1½ cups grated/shredded
   firm mozzarella cheese
a handful of fresh basil leaves
cracked black pepper, to serve
good-quality balsamic vinegar,
   to drizzle (optional)
4 slices of ciabatta/Italian bread,
   toasted, to serve

SERVES 4

Heat the oil in a medium-large frying pan/skillet set over medium heat and sauté the onion until softened. Add the tomatoes, salt and pepper and continue to cook for about 5 minutes until the tomatoes begin to soften and release their juices.

Use a large spoon to create 4 evenly spaced depressions in the tomato mixture. Crack an egg into each depression, cover the frying pan/skillet and cook for 3–4 minutes until the whites have set and the yolks are almost cooked to desired doneness.

Sprinkle the cheese over the top, cover with a lid and cook just until the cheese is melted. Scatter over the basil and cracked black pepper and serve with the toasted bread on the side.

Serve with a Classic Negroni recipe on page 41

FIG, BLUE CHEESE & ROCKET PIZZETTE

FIGS HAVE A NATURAL AFFINITY WITH BLUE CHEESE, AND ROCKET/ARUGULA BALANCES THE SWEET AND THE SALT WITH A PEPPERY KICK. THE PIZZETTE BASES ARE SMEARED WITH ROBIOLINO – A SOFT, MILD CHEESE NOT UNLIKE PHILADELPHIA BUT WITH A LESS PRONOUNCED FLAVOUR.

300 g/10 oz. Robiolino (or other buttery cream cheese)
400 g/14 oz. Gorgonzola
4–5 ripe fresh figs (ripe but not too soft)
a generous handful of fresh rocket/arugula

PIZZETTE DOUGH
500 g/3½ cups Italian '00' flour
10 g/2 teaspoons salt
5 g/1 teaspoon fresh yeast
250 ml/1 cup warm water

MARGHERITA PIZZETTE (OPTIONAL)
120 ml/4 oz. passata/strained tomatoes
½ teaspoon dried oregano
1 tablespoon extra virgin olive oil, plus extra to drizzle
400 g/14 oz. buffalo mozzarella
fresh basil leaves, to garnish

3 large baking sheets, floured

MAKES 8

Start by making the pizzette dough. Put the flour into a large mixing bowl and stir in the salt. In a separate bowl, stir the yeast and water together until the yeast has dissolved and then mix it into the flour. Bring everything together to form a soft dough. Leave the mixture to rest for 10 minutes, then lightly knead the dough, cover and leave to rest for 1 hour, somewhere not too warm.

Lightly knead the dough a second time and leave for a further 1 hour. Knead the dough a third time, then cut into 8 pieces. Roll the dough out into 20-cm/8-inch circles, making sure the bases are really thin. Lay them on the prepared baking sheets and leave for 30 minutes while you preheat the oven to its highest setting, usually 230°C (450°F) Gas 8.

Spread the bases with a thin layer of Robiolino. Arrange small nuggets of Gorgonzola evenly over the top and bake in the preheated oven for 8–10 minutes, until the bases are crisp and golden. Slice or quarter the fresh figs and arrange them over the pizzette. Garnish with fresh rocket/arugula and serve at once.

MARGHERITA PIZZETTE

Prepare the bases as above, mix the passata/strained tomatoes, oregano and oil together, and spread a thin layer over each base. Tear the mozzarella into pieces and arrange over each pizzette. Drizzle with olive oil and bake as above. Garnish with fresh basil leaves and serve at once.

Serve with an *Aperol Spritz* recipe on page 41

CAPONATA WITH GRILLED POLENTA & WHIPPED FETA

700 g/7 cups (about 2) diced aubergines/eggplants
125 ml/½ cup olive oil
1 large onion, diced
1 garlic clove, crushed
1 red plus 1 orange or yellow (bell) pepper, deseeded and diced
2 celery stalks, cut on an angle into 2-cm/¾-inch slices
4 tablespoons red wine vinegar
1 x 400-g/14-oz. can chopped tomatoes
2 teaspoons caster/ granulated sugar
35 g/⅓ cup green olives, pitted and halved
1 tablespoon capers, rinsed and drained
20 g/¼ cup flaked/slivered almonds, lightly toasted
sea salt and freshly ground black pepper
a handful of freshly chopped flat-leaf parsley, to serve

GRILLED POLENTA
200 g/1⅓ cups quick-cook polenta/cornmeal
80 g/5 tablespoons butter
50 g/1 cup grated Parmesan cheese

WHIPPED FETA
250 g/2 cups feta cheese
60 ml/¼ cup Greek yogurt
60 ml/¼ cup extra virgin olive oil
1 tablespoon freshly squeezed lemon juice

an 18 x 25-cm/7 x 10-inch baking pan, greased
a baking sheet, oiled

SERVES 6

CAPONATA IMPROVES WITH AGE AND IS EXTREMELY VERSATILE. IT MAKES A GREAT VEGETARIAN BRUNCH DISH, SERVED HERE WITH GRILLED POLENTA IN PLACE OF BREAD.

Put the aubergine/eggplant in a colander and sprinkle with salt. Leave for 30 minutes, then rinse under cold running water and pat dry with paper towels.

Heat the oil in a large, heavy-based saucepan over a medium heat. Add the aubergine/eggplant and fry for 5–8 minutes, until golden brown, stirring occasionally. Remove from the pan and set aside. Add the onion to the same pan and fry for 5 minutes, or until softened (you may need to add a little more oil). Add the garlic and cook for another minute before adding the peppers and celery. Cook for 5 minutes, then add the vinegar and stir to deglaze the pan. Stir in the tomatoes and sugar and simmer for 5–10 minutes.

Return the aubergine/eggplant to the pan with the olives and capers, and mix well. Cook for a further 5 minutes. Remove from the heat, season and stir in the almonds.

To make the polenta, bring 1 litre/4 cups of salted water to the boil in a medium saucepan or pot. Gradually pour in the polenta/cornmeal while stirring continuously with a wooden spoon. Reduce the heat and keep stirring for about 5 minutes. Remove from the heat and stir in the butter and the Parmesan. Adjust the seasoning as necessary. Working quickly, spread the polenta mix evenly across the prepared baking pan to a layer 2 cm/¾ inch deep. Set aside to cool.

For the whipped feta, crumble the feta into a food processor and pulse together with the yogurt until smooth. Add the oil and mix until it becomes very soft. Add the lemon juice and put in the fridge.

Preheat the grill/broiler to a medium heat. Tip the set polenta onto a board and cut into six rectangles. Cut these in half diagonally to give you 12 triangles. Place the polenta on the prepared baking sheet and set under the grill/broiler to cook for about 10 minutes, or until golden. Turn the polenta and grill the other side in the same way. Reheat the caponata over a medium heat and stir through the parsley. Heap the caponata onto plates, top with the grilled polenta and a dollop of whipped feta. Season and serve.

Serve with a *Tintaretta*, recipe on page 40.

RICOTTA PANCAKES WITH CHERRY COMPOTE

THESE RICOTTA PANCAKES ARE LIGHT YET CREAMY AT THE SAME TIME AND MAKE FOR A DECIDEDLY LUXURIOUS BRUNCH, DISH ESPECIALLY WHEN SERVED WITH A DEEP PURPLE CHERRY COMPOTE THAT CONTRASTS IN BOTH FLAVOUR AND COLOUR.

200 g/scant 1 cup ricotta cheese
200 ml/¾ cup full-fat/whole milk
2 eggs, separated
1 teaspoon freshly squeezed
   lemon juice
140 g/1 generous cup plain/
   all-purpose flour
½ tablespoon baking powder
1 tablespoon caster/granulated
   sugar
butter, for shallow frying

CHERRY COMPOTE
400 g/14 oz. fresh cherries,
   destalked
30 g/2½ tablespoons caster/
   superfine sugar
a squeeze of fresh lemon juice

SERVES 4

To make the cherry compote, stone/pit each cherry by squashing it with the flat side of a knife until you hit the stone/pit, then rip open the cherry, remove the stone/pit and throw the cherry flesh straight into a saucepan. Add the sugar, lemon juice and 2 tablespoons of cold water to the pan. Bring to a boil over a medium heat, then reduce to a simmer and cook for 10–15 minutes, until the liquid thickens and the cherries are soft, adding more water if it starts to catch during cooking. Spoon into a bowl, cover and set aside.

To make the pancakes, put the ricotta, milk, egg yolks and lemon juice in a large bowl and mix until well combined. Combine the flour, baking powder and sugar and then fold into the ricotta mixture. Finally, loosen the egg whites with a fork (no need to whisk them) and fold into the ricotta mixture.

Heat a knob/pat of butter in a frying pan/skillet set over a medium heat. Once it has melted pour in about half a ladleful of batter; this will make 10-cm/4-inch diameter pancakes, about 10–12 of them. Leave to cook for a few minutes, until you see bubbles appearing on the surface – this is your signal to flip the pancake over. Use a fish slice to do this and cook for 2–3 minutes more. Once cooked remove from the pan. Repeat until all the batter has been used, keeping the pancakes warm in a low oven or on a plate and covered with foil as you go.

Stack the pancakes on serving plates, spoon over some of the cherry compote and serve while still warm.

Aperol Spritz

The Aperol Spritz is one of the most popular aperitif cocktails in Italy. Just Aperol, prosecco and club soda – it is as easy to make as it is to drink so a great choice for brunch.

200 ml/¾ cup Aperol
600 ml/2½ cups Prosecco
300–400 ml/1¼–1½ cups club
    soda or sparkling water
ice cubes

SERVES 4

Put lots of cubed (never crushed) ice into four large, chilled wine glasses. Divide the Aperol and Prosecco between the glasses, then top up with club soda. Serve at once.

Tintoretto

The pomegranate-spiked Tintoretto is a pretty and delicious cocktail from the legendary Venetian institution Caffè Florian in St. Mark's Square.

140 ml/½ cup pomegranate juice
600 ml/2½ cups chilled Prosecco

SERVES 4

Pour the pomegranate juice into four Champagne flutes, then slowly top up with chilled Prosecco. Serve at once.

Pictured on page 37.

Classic Negroni

Composed of gin, sweet vermouth and Campari, the Negroni is the classic Italian drink. It is strong, bitter and deeply sophisticated...

180 ml/¾ cup Campari
180 ml/¾ cup gin
60 ml/¼ cup Cinzano Rosso or
    other red vermouth
orange slices, to serve
crushed or cubed ice

SERVES 4

Fill four rocks glasses or tumblers with ice. Divide the Campari between the glasses, then the gin. Add the Cinzano Rosso and stir. Drop a slice of orange into each glass and serve at once.

Pictured on page 33.

Strawberry & Basil Bellini

Adapt a classic Bellini (see below) to the changing seasons – fresh strawberry and basil makes a delicious summer variation.

20 ripe strawberries
4 teaspoons white sugar
480 ml/2 cups Prosecco
a large handful of fresh basil
   leaves

SERVES 4

Whizz the strawberries and sugar together in a blender to make a purée. Pour the purée into a large jug/pitcher, add a little of the Prosecco and the basil. Bash with a blunt object until lots of flavour has been released. Pour the mixture through a strainer into chilled flute glasses. Pour over the remaining Prosecco and stir gently. Serve at once.

Classic White Peach Bellini

The Bellini was invented by Giuseppe Cipriani at the celebrated Harry's Bar in Venice around 80 years ago. It's a mixture of fresh peach juice and Prosecco.

40 ml/3 tablespoons freshly made
   peach purée (see note on
   page 140)
480 ml/2 cups Prosecco

SERVES 4

Pour the peach purée into four chilled Champagne flutes. Pour in the Prosecco and stir gently. Serve at once.

Pear Bellini

A variation that works well in the winter months.

200 ml/¾ cup pear purée
480 ml/2 cups Prosecco

SERVES 4

Pour the pear purée into the chilled glasses. Pour in the Prosecco and stir gently. Serve immediately.

Pictured on page 153.

PARISIAN

PRETZEL CROISSANTS

THE PRETZEL CROISSANT IS A WONDERFUL TWIST ON A TRADITIONAL FRENCH PASTRY. IT DOES NEED TO BE PREPARED IN ADVANCE AND BAKED ON THE MORNING OF YOUR BRUNCH, BUT IT IS WELL WORTH THE EFFORT!

500 ml/2 cups cold milk
2 tablespoons runny honey
600 g/4½ cups bread flour, plus more for dusting
65 g/½ cup pastry flour
100 g/½ cup granulated sugar
40 g/1½ oz. fresh yeast, crumbled
1 tablespoon plus 1½ teaspoons sea salt
575 g/5 sticks unsalted butter, very cold
1 large egg, lightly beaten
sea salt and white sesame seeds to sprinkle over the dough

electric food mixer with dough hook

MAKES 10–12

Stir the milk and honey together in a large jug/pitcher. In an electric food mixer fitted with a dough hook, combine the bread flour, pastry flour, sugar, yeast and salt. Add the milk and honey and mix on a low speed until the dough is just coming together, about 2½ minutes. Turn out onto a lightly floured work surface and knead for about 45 seconds, forming a smooth ball. Wrap in clingfilm/plastic wrap and refrigerate for 1 hour.

Meanwhile, unwrap the butter and lay the pieces side by side on clingfilm/plastic wrap. Sprinkle the butter with bread flour, then pound the butter with a rolling pin until the flour is incorporated into the butter. Roll into a 20-cm/8-in. square. Wrap in clingfilm/plastic wrap and refrigerate for 1 hour.

Remove the dough ball from the fridge, unwrap and place on a lightly floured surface. Roll into a 40 x 25-cm/16 x 10-in. rectangle, 1.25 cm/½ in. thick. The short side should face you. Brush off excess flour. Place the chilled butter on top of the dough.

Starting at the farthest side from you, fold the top half of the rectangle over the butter. Repeat with the side closest to you, overlapping. Flip the dough and butter mixture over, with seams facing down. Roll the dough until the butter and dough come together. Then roll the dough out into another 40 x 25-cm/16 x 10-in. rectangle. Fold the dough in thirds, like a letter. Wrap in clingfilm/plastic wrap and refrigerate for 1 hour.

Repeat the rolling and folding twice more, starting with the flap opening on the right, and refrigerate for at least 1 hour between turns. After the third roll, refrigerate for 6–8 hours or overnight.

Place the dough on a lightly floured work surface and roll to a 76 x 40-cm/30 x 16-in. rectangle. Using a pizza cutter, cut in half lengthwise to form two 76 x 20-cm/30 x 8-in. rectangles. Place one of the pieces on top of the other, lining up the edges. Cut into triangles; each should have a 10-cm/4-inch bottom. Cut a slit into the centre of the base of each triangle. Place the triangles side by side on a clean work surface.

Stretch the lower half of each triangle, expanding the slit, then fold the inner corners formed by the slit towards the outer sides of the triangle, pressing down to seal the croissant. Using a fingertip, roll the base of the triangle away from you, upwards. Stretch the dough slightly outwards as you roll. The tip should be tucked under. Place the 2 ends towards you to form a crescent.

Transfer to a baking sheet, 5 cm/2 in. apart. Cover with clingfilm/plastic wrap and let rise in a warm spot for 1 hour. They will double in size and become spongy.

Preheat the oven to 200°C (400°F) Gas 6. Brush the croissants with egg wash and sprinkle with salt and sesame seeds. Bake for 20–25 minutes, rotating half-way through until the croissants are puffed and golden. Cool on a wire rack before serving.

PARIS-STYLE EGGS BENEDICT

THIS VARIANT ON A TRADITIONAL FRENCH BREAKFAST COMES
WITH BACON, BRIE AND POACHED EGGS, ALL ASSEMBLED ON TOP
OF A PRETZEL CROISSANT (OR YOU CAN USE A FRESHLY BAKED CLASSIC
CROISSANT FOR SPEED) AND DRIZZLED WITH HOLLANDAISE SAUCE. THIS
DECADENT AND DELICIOUS DISH MAKES THE PERFECT SUNDAY BRUNCH.

60 g/½ stick butter
4 slices of bacon
2 teaspoons white or rice vinegar
8 slices of Brie cheese
4 eggs
4 Pretzel Croissants (see page 47),
    optional
butter, for spreading
dash of Tabasco sauce (optional)
a couple of sprigs of flat-leaf
    parsley, chopped, to garnish
freshly ground black pepper

HOLLANDAISE SAUCE
140 g/1¼ sticks unsalted butter
3 egg yolks
1 tablespoon freshly squeezed
    lemon juice
½ teaspoon salt

SERVES 4

To make the hollandaise sauce, melt the butter in a small saucepan. Put the egg yolks, lemon juice and salt in a blender and blend on medium to medium-high speed for 25 seconds or until the eggs lighten in colour. Change the blender speed to the lowest setting and very slowly, pour in the hot butter and continue to blend. Add salt and lemon juice to taste. Transfer to a small jug/pitcher.

Melt some butter in a large frying pan/skillet on a low to medium heat, and when the pan is hot, add the bacon, turning it occasionally until cooked.

While the bacon is cooking, fill a large saucepan with water and bring to the boil. Add the vinegar and let it come to a boil again. After the water boils, reduce the heat to a simmer.

Next, poach the eggs. The easiest way is to do one egg at a time. Crack the egg into a small bowl and slip it into the barely simmering water. Once the egg begins to solidify, slip in the next egg and so on until you have all 4 cooking. Turn the heat off, cover the pan with a lid and let the eggs sit for 3–4 minutes, depending on how runny you like your eggs. Starting with the first egg you cracked, gently lift them out with a slotted spoon and set them down in a bowl or on a plate.

Toast and butter the croissants. Top with the bacon, 2 slices of Brie and a poached egg. Sprinkle on Tabasco sauce if desired. Pour the hollandaise sauce over the top and garnish with flat-leaf parsley and ground black pepper to taste.

Serve with a Pamini *recipe on page 57*

BUTTERMILK PANCAKES WITH SALMON & HORSERADISH CREAM

FOR AN INDULGENT BRUNCH, TRY THESE SIMPLE YET DELICIOUS FLUFFY BUTTERMILK PANCAKES SEASONED WITH CHIVES AND TOPPED WITH THICK SLICES OF SMOKED SALMON AND HORSERADISH CREAM – OH LA LA!

170 g/1⅓ cups self-raising/rising flour, sifted
1 teaspoon baking powder
2 eggs, separated
200 ml/⅔ cup buttermilk
2 teaspoons caster/granulated sugar
1 tablespoon finely chopped chives, plus extra for sprinkling
100 ml/⅓ cup milk
250 ml/1 cup crème fraîche
1 heaped tablespoon creamed horseradish
1–2 tablespoons butter, for frying
400 g/2½ cups smoked salmon, to serve
1 lemon, sliced into wedges
sea salt and freshly ground black pepper

a large frying pan/skillet or griddle

SERVES 4

To make the pancake batter, put the flour, baking powder, egg yolks, buttermilk, sugar and chives in a large mixing bowl and whisk together. Season well with salt and pepper, then gradually add the milk until the batter is smooth and pourable.

In a separate bowl, whisk the egg whites to stiff peaks. Gently fold the whisked egg whites into the batter mixture using a spatula. Cover and put in the fridge to rest for 30 minutes.

For the horseradish cream, whisk together the crème fraîche and horseradish in a small bowl and season with salt and pepper.

When you are ready to serve, remove the batter mixture from the fridge and stir once. Put a little butter in a large frying pan/skillet set over a medium heat. Allow the butter to melt and coat the base of the pan, then ladle small amounts of the rested batter into the pan, leaving a little space between each. Cook until the underside of each pancake is golden brown and a few bubbles start to appear on the top – this will take about 2–3 minutes. Turn the pancake over using a spatula and cook on the other side until golden brown.

Serve the pancakes warm, topped with a generous spoon of the horseradish cream, slices of smoked salmon and wedge of lemon to squeeze over the top. Sprinkle with extra chopped chives.

Serve with a chilled glass of Champagne

FRENCH TOAST WITH ASPARAGUS & HOLLANDAISE

HOLLANDAISE SAUCE AND ASPARAGUS ARE ONE OF LIFE'S SWEETEST LUXURIES. THIS VERSION OF THE CLASSIC SAUCE USES ORANGE AND BASIL VINEGAR IN THE REDUCTION INSTEAD OF THE MORE USUAL LEMON. IF YOU DO NOT HAVE BASIL VINEGAR, YOU CAN ADD 2–3 BASIL LEAVES TO THE REDUCTION OR JUST REPLACE IT WITH WHITE WINE OR SHERRY VINEGAR.

14–16 fresh asparagus spears, trimmed
3 eggs
4 slices of white bread
sea salt and freshly ground black and pink pepper

ORANGE HOLLANDAISE SAUCE
80 ml/scant ⅓ cup basil vinegar or white wine vinegar
1 shallot, finely chopped
1 teaspoon black peppercorns
grated zest of 1 unwaxed orange
3 egg yolks
175 g/1 stick plus 3 tablespoons butter, melted, plus extra for frying

a large frying pan/skillet or griddle

SERVES 2

Begin by making the sauce. Put the vinegar, chopped shallot, peppercorns and orange zest in a saucepan set over a medium heat and simmer until the mixture reduces and becomes syrupy – you should be left with 1–2 tablespoons of liquid. Remove from the heat and strain through a sieve/strainer over a bowl to remove and discard the zest, peppercorns and shallots. Put the bowl over a pan of simmering water on a very low heat and add the egg yolks. Whisk until the mixture is very thick, then add the melted butter 1 spoonful at a time, whisking continuously. The important thing is to keep the heat very gentle so that the eggs do not overcook. If the sauce splits, add 1 tablespoon of ice cold water or an ice cube and whisk well to re-emulsify the sauce.

While the hollandaise is cooking, put the asparagus in a steaming basket over a pan of boiling water, sprinkle with a little sea salt and steam for about 3–4 minutes until it is soft but still has bite.

For the French toast, beat the eggs in a mixing bowl and season well with salt and pepper. Melt the butter in a large frying pan/skillet set over a medium heat until the butter begins to foam. Soak each slice in the beaten egg mixture on one side for a few seconds, then turn over and soak the other side. The slices should be fully coated in egg, but not too soggy – it is best to soak one slice at a time. Put each slice straight in the pan before soaking and cooking the next slice.

Cook for 2–3 minutes on each side until the egg is cooked and the slices are lightly golden brown. Keep the toasts warm while you cook the remaining slices.

Serve 2 slices of French toast per person, topped with asparagus and a generous spoonful of the hollandaise sauce.

Serve with a *Kir Royale*, recipe on page 57

SALADE DE CHÈVRE WITH EDIBLE FLOWERS

WHAT SAYS PARIS MORE THAN SALADE DE CHÈVRE? THE RADICCHIO ADDS A COMPLEXITY AND A SLIGHT BITTERNESS. THIS PAIRS WELL WITH THE WALNUTS AND THE CREAMINESS OF THE GOAT'S CHEESE, MAKING IT THE PERFECT BRUNCH ACCOMPANIMENT.

120 g/¾ cup walnut halves, toasted
2 tablespoons sherry vinegar
60 ml/4 tablespoons walnut oil
2 teaspoons Dijon mustard
a drizzle of honey
240 g/1½ cups goat's cheese
1 sourdough baguette, cut diagonally into 12 slices
12 sprigs of fresh thyme
1 head butter lettuce
1 radicchio (pink, if in season)
1 small red gem lettuce
a punnet of edible flowers

SERVES 6

Preheat the oven to 180°C (350°F) Gas 4.

Spread the walnuts over a baking sheet. Bake in the preheated oven for 5 minutes or until lightly toasted. Set aside to cool.

Whisk the vinegar, oil, mustard and honey in a bowl and set aside.

Preheat the grill/broiler to medium-high. Cut the goat's cheese into 12 slices. Place the bread on a baking sheet and cook under the grill/broiler for 1 minute on each side or until light and golden. Turn and top each slice with a piece of goat's cheese. Spread the cheese to the edges of the toast and top with the thyme. Cook under the grill/broiler for 2 minutes or until the cheese softens.

Meanwhile, tear the salad leaves into a bowl and mix well. Lightly drizzle with half of the dressing and place onto 6 plates or a large platter. Top with goat's cheese toasts and walnuts, then drizzle over the rest of the dressing and top with edible flowers. Serve at once.

Serve with The Pink & The Green, recipe on page 58

Pamini

The tartness of the grapefruit juice works well with the Champagne as a refreshing brunch cocktail, kickstarting your appetite.

300 ml/1¼ cups freshly squeezed grapefruit juice, strained
1 x 750-ml/25-oz. bottle of Champagne or crèmant
1 small grapefruit, cut into 6 small slices, to garnish (optional)

SERVES 6

Divide the grapefruit juice between 6 Champagne flutes and top up with Champagne. Garnish with a slice of grapefruit, it liked, and serve at once.

Pictured opposite.

Kir Royale

This French cocktail is the ultimate elegant cocktail and evokes thoughts of Paris.

60 ml/4 tablespoons crème de cassis
1 x 750-ml/25-oz. bottle of Champagne or crèmant
6 fresh blackberries, to garnish (optional)

SERVES 6

Pour 10 ml/2 teaspoons of the crème de cassis into each of 6 Champagne flutes and top up with Champagne. Garnish each glass with a blackberry, if liked, and serve at once.

Pictured on page 49.

Mimosa

A bartender at the Hotel Ritz Paris is thought to have invented the Mimosa around 1925. But whoever came up with it, it was a devilishly good idea and a brunch classic.

60 ml/4 tablespoons Grand Marnier or Cointreau
1 x 750-ml/25-oz. bottle of Champagne or crèmant
300 ml/1¼ cups freshly squeezed orange juice, strained

SERVES 6

Pour 10 ml/2 teaspoons of the Grand Marnier into each of 6 Champagne flutes and half fill with Champagne. Top up with the strained orange juice and stir gently. Serve at once.

The Pink & The Green

A fragrant and delicate combination of rosé wine,
elderflower liqueur and a homemade cucumber syrup.

1 x 750-ml/25-oz. bottle of ripe,
  fruity rosé, well chilled
250 ml/1 cup St-Germain
  elderflower liqueur (or
  elderflower cordial for
  a lower alcohol content)
125 ml/½ cup freshly squeezed
  lemon juice
45 ml/3 tablespoons Cucumber
  Syrup (see right)
30 ml/2 tablespoons rosewater
1–1½ litres/4–6 cups Fever-Tree
  elderflower Indian tonic water,
  well chilled
cucumber slices and lemon
  wheels
edible rose petals, to garnish
ice cubes

SERVES 6–8

Pour the rosé, elderflower liqueur, lemon juice, cucumber syrup and rosewater into a large punch bowl. Add plenty of ice cubes to chill, then add elderflower tonic to taste. Follow with the cucumber and lemon slices and stir.

Scatter over the rose petals just before serving. Ladle into ice-cube-filled white wine glasses, adding a little of the fruit and edible rose petals to each glass. Serve at once.

CUCUMBER SYRUP

Put 250 ml/1 cup of water in a small saucepan with 225 g/1 cup white granulated sugar. Bring to the boil and let simmer for a minute until clear and slightly thickened. Take off the heat and add the chopped flesh and skin of about half a medium cucumber. Leave to cool and transfer to a clean screw-top jar. Refrigerate (for a few hours or overnight if possible) to marinate, then strain the syrup, discard the cucumber pieces, and return the syrup to the jar. The syrup will keep in the fridge for up to 3 weeks.

TEX-MEX

STEAK & EGG BREAKFAST TACOS

IT'S USUALLY THE BREAKFAST BURRITO THAT STEALS THE SHOW WHEN IT COMES TO TEX-MEX BRUNCHES, BUT THESE STEAK AND EGG TACOS ARE NOTHING TO SCOFF AT. FRIED EGGS, STEAK AND KETCHUP KEEP THIS TASTY DISH SIMPLE AND HEARTY.

2 steaks
1–2 teaspoons olive oil, to season the steaks
8 eggs
8 small corn tortillas/tacos
vegetable oil, for shallow frying
tomato ketchup, for topping
salt and freshly ground black pepper

a cast-iron frying pan/skillet

SERVES 4

To cook the steaks, preheat the oven to 200°C (400°F) Gas 6 and heat a cast-iron frying pan/skillet (or other heavy-based ovenproof pan) over a medium heat.

Season the steaks with salt and pepper, using your fingers to rub the seasoning and about 1 teaspoon of olive oil into both sides of each steak. Add the steaks to the preheated pan and cook for 1–2 minutes on each side before sliding the pan into the preheated oven. Cook the steaks for a further 2–3 minutes for medium to medium-well done. Remove the pan from the oven and let the steaks rest for 2 minutes before slicing them into thin strips.

While the steaks rest, fry the eggs. Set a small non-stick frying pan/skillet over medium heat and add a little vegetable oil. Break in 1 egg. Season with a little salt and fry until the white is set. Remove to a warm plate and repeat with the remaining eggs.

If you can double-task, heat the tortillas, either by holding them directly over a gas flame with metal tongs, or in a dry cast-iron frying pan/skillet set over high heat. You want them to be puffed and a little blistered.

Place an egg on top of each tortilla and spoon the sliced steak on top of the egg. Top with ketchup and serve immediately.

Serve with Majitas with Lime Sea Salt, recipe on page 73

CHORIZO NACHO SKILLET WITH HOMEMADE TORTILLA CHIPS

USING SPICY CHORIZO SAUSAGE, SCRAMBLED EGG AND A BLEND OF THREE CHEESES, THIS HEARTY RECIPE MAKES A TASTY SHARING DISH. THE TEXTURES ARE FANTASTIC AND THE DISH HAS PLENTY OF SPICY TEX-MEX FLAIR.

450 g/1 lb. chorizo sausage
½ white onion, chopped
5 eggs, beaten
4 ripe tomatoes, chopped
2 jarred jalapeño peppers, sliced
225 g/8 oz. pre-packaged 'Mexican blend' grated/shredded cheese or a mixture of freshly grated/shredded mature/sharp Cheddar, mild Cheddar/Colby and Gouda/Monterey Jack
125 ml/½ cup sour cream

HOMEMADE TORTILLA CHIPS
1 packet soft flour or corn tortillas, as preferred
2 tablespoons vegetable oil

a baking sheet, lightly greased
a cast-iron frying pan/skillet

SERVES 4

Preheat the oven to 180°C (350°F) Gas 4.

First make the tortilla chips. Using a pastry brush, paint a very light coating of oil on one side of each tortilla. Stack the tortillas greased side up in an even pile. Divide the stack in two and cut the tortillas into quarters and then into eighths. Separate the chips and arrange them oiled-side up on the prepared baking sheet.

Bake the chips in the preheated oven for about 10 minutes or until they are crisp and just beginning to brown slightly. Remove them from the oven, but you can leave the oven on if you are ready to make up the frying pan/skillet.

Cook the chorizo in a frying pan/skillet for about 5 minutes over a medium heat until crumbled and evenly browned. Drain and set aside. Cook the onion in the same frying pan/skillet until soft, then stir in the eggs and scramble with the onion. Mix in the tomatoes and continue to cook and stir until the eggs are nearly set. Remove from the heat.

Spread a layer of tortilla chips into a medium cast-iron (or ovenproof) frying pan/skillet. Scatter the chorizo and the scrambled egg mixture over the chips. Top with jalapeño slices and cover with the grated/shredded cheese.

Bake in the preheated oven for 7–10 minutes, until the cheese is melted. Serve hot and eat with your fingers!

Serve with Margaritas with Jalapeñas, *recipe on page 72*

BAKED EGG 'HOPPERS' WITH TOMATO RELISH, CHORIZO & AVOCADO

THESE FUN HOPPER-STYLE PANCAKES ARE MADE AS NORMAL AND THEN PRESSED INTO PANS TO MAKE SHALLOW BOWLS FOR THE BAKED EGGS TO SIT IN. THEY ARE THEN BAKED AND SERVED WITH CHORIZO, AVOCADO AND A SMOKY TOMATO RELISH.

100 g/¾ cup plain/all-purpose flour
4 tablespoons chickpea/gram flour
2 teaspoons baking powder
pinch of salt
250 ml/1 cup plus 1 tablespoon buttermilk
1 egg, beaten

FILLING
olive oil, for frying
6 eggs
1 avocado
150 g/5½ oz. chorizo, thinly sliced
50 g/scant 1 cup baby spinach

TOMATO RELISH
3 tomatoes, halved, deseeded and chopped
½ onion, finely chopped
2 tablespoons red wine vinegar
2 tablespoons dark brown sugar
¼ teaspoon smoked paprika
pinch of cayenne pepper
sea salt and freshly ground black pepper

MAKES 6

Start by making the relish. Place all the ingredients into a saucepan and season with salt and pepper. Bring to the boil and simmer, uncovered, for about 15–20 minutes, stirring occasionally, until thickened. Set aside and leave to cool.

Grease six 8 x 12-cm/3 x 5-in. pie pans with olive oil and line them with baking parchment. Set the lined pans on a large baking sheet. Preheat the oven to 180°C (350°F) Gas 4.

To make the pancake batter, sift the plain/all-purpose flour, chickpea/gram flour, baking powder and salt into a large mixing bowl. Make a well in the centre and beat in the buttermilk and egg to make a smooth batter.

Lightly oil a pancake pan and place over a medium heat. Once hot, add about 80 ml/⅓ cup of the batter and tilt the pan, allowing the batter to spread across in an even layer. Cook for about 2–3

minutes until the base is browned and the top set. Remove from the pan and very carefully transfer to one of the prepared pie pans, pressing it down to fit snugly inside in a bowl shape.

Repeat for the rest of the batter and pancakes (you should be able to make about 6 from the batter). Crack an egg into each pancake and bake in the preheated oven for 8–10 minutes until the eggs are just set.

Meanwhile, peel, stone/pit and slice the avocado and set aside. Heat a tablespoon of oil in a small frying pan/skillet over a medium heat and gently fry the chorizo slices for 2–3 minutes until golden and fragrant.

Remove the baked egg hoppers from the oven and top each one with a little fried chorizo, avocado slices, spinach and a spoonful of the tomato relish. Drizzle over any chorizo cooking oil and serve.

MAPLE-CURED
BACON & TOMATO SANDWICH

8 slices sourdough bread
2 tablespoons mayonnaise
4 eggs, cooked on both sides
    (optional)
8 tomato slices
4 slices Cheddar cheese (optional)
maple-cured bacon (see below),
    allow 2 slices per sandwich
a handful of rocket/arugula
sea salt and freshly ground
    black pepper
sweet pickles and sweet potato
    fries, to serve

MAPLE-CURED BACON:
140 g/1 cup sea salt
400 g/2 cups brown sugar
    (preferably soft dark brown
    sugar)
320 g/1 cup pure maple syrup
2.25–4.5 kg/5–10 lbs. pork belly,
    washed and patted dry, with
    the skin left on

SERVES 4

THERE'S NO TURNING BACK ONCE YOU'VE TRIED HOMEMADE MAPLE-CURED BACON, ALTHOUGH YOU WILL NEED TO PREPARE IT A WEEK IN ADVANCE. WHEN IT'S READY, JUST TRY TO STOP YOURSELF FRYING UP THE WHOLE LOT AND WORKING YOUR WAY THROUGH IT WITH STICKY FINGERS AND GUILTY PLEASURE.

Curing bacon at home takes a while, but it's really worth it. In a medium bowl, combine the salt, sugar and maple syrup. Rub the mixture over the pork belly on both sides. Place the pork in a large resealable plastic bag with a zip and seal tightly. Refrigerate and let cure for 7 days, turning once a day.

After 7 days, the bacon will be cured. Cut off a small piece and fry it to test the saltiness of the bacon. If the bacon doesn't taste too salty after being cooked, you are ready to proceed. If the bacon tastes too salty, soak the remaining pork belly in cold water for 1 hour.

Once the bacon is ready to cook, carefully slice it into strips of the desired thickness. Fry it for 3–4 minutes per side, until it reaches the crispiness that you like. Fry the eggs, if using.

Assemble the sandwiches with slices of sourdough bread, mayonnaise, eggs (if using), tomatoes, Cheddar cheese (if using), rocket/arugula, salt and pepper. Serve with sweet pickles and sweet potato fries.

Serve with a *Beergarita Granita,* recipe on page 73, or a Corona

CHURROS WITH MOCHA DIP

A POPULAR TREAT IN MEXICO, TRADITIONALLY MADE WITH BUTTER AND EGGS, THIS RECIPE IS USEFULLY VEGAN AND DAIRY-FREE BUT STILL HAS THE DESIRED CRISP GOLDEN EXTERIOR AND FLUFFY CENTRE. SERVE IN A HAZE OF CINNAMON SUGAR AND WITH AN ESPRESSO WHIPPED INTO A CHOCOLATE DIP ON THE SIDE.

1 tablespoon ground cinnamon
2 tablespoons caster/superfine sugar, plus an extra pinch, divided
140 g/1 generous cup plain/all-purpose flour
1 teaspoon baking powder
60 ml/¼ cup olive oil
vegetable oil, for deep frying

MOCHA DIP
60 ml/¼ cup almond milk
90 g/3 oz. vegan dark/bittersweet chocolate (minimum 70% cocoa), broken into pieces
30 ml/2 tablespoons freshly made espresso coffee, cooled

a piping/pastry bag with a 2-cm/¾-inch star nozzle/tip, or disposable piping bag (although this won't give the signature grooved surface)

SERVES 4

Mix the cinnamon and sugar together in a small bowl and set aside.

Combine the flour with the baking powder and add the extra pinch of sugar. Pour 250 ml/1 cup cold water into a saucepan and set over a medium heat. Add the olive oil, bring the mixture to the boil, then remove it from the heat. Immediately shoot in the flour mixture and beat with a wooden spoon until it comes together; stop as soon as it starts to hold together and don't overwork it. It will be a sticky, slightly messy looking dough – and that's exactly what you want. Spoon the dough into the prepared piping/pastry bag and push it down into the bag to remove any air-filled gaps.

Pour the vegetable oil into a large, heavy-based saucepan set over a medium heat. The oil is ready when a small piece of bread dropped into the oil sizzles but takes 1 minute to turn golden.

Line a plate or tray with paper towels. Carefully pipe the churros dough directly into the hot oil. Traditionally churros are straight logs about 12–15 cm/5–6 inches long. If using a nozzle, just snip the batter into lengths with scissors as you pipe; if using a disposable bag just pinch the end of it when you want to break the piping.

Deep fry for about 5 minutes, until crisp and just starting to turn golden (these churros will remain a little paler than regular ones). Use a slotted spoon to transfer the cooked churros onto the lined plate or tray. Once slightly cooled, sprinkle over the cinnamon sugar.

To make the mocha dip, put the almond milk and chocolate in a bowl and microwave for 30 seconds, stir to combine and mix in the coffee. Alternatively, heat the milk over a medium heat in a small saucepan and once it starts to bubble drop in the chocolate and whisk together until the chocolate melts. Finish by adding the shot of coffee.

Serve the warm churros as soon as possible with the mocha dip on the side for dunking.

Margaritas With Jalapeños

This is definitely great for an all-day brunch crowd! Refreshing with a touch of heat from the addition of the jalapeño pepper.

300 ml/1¼ cups silver tequila
freshly squeezed juice from
    6 limes, plus 2 limes cut into
    wedges, to serve
45 ml/3 tablespoons agave syrup
5 cups ice cubes
3 tablespoons fine sea salt
1 fresh jalapeño chilli/chile, sliced

SERVES 6

Put the tequila, lime juice, agave syrup and ice in a blender and blend until smooth. Pour the salt onto a plate and moisten the rims of 6 glasses with a lime wedge. Dip the rim of each glass into the salt and pour in the margaritas. Serve with lime wedges and a slice of jalapeño in each glass.

Pictured opposite and on page 65.

Mojito With Lime Sea Salt

Serve this in a pitcher, but dust each rim of your glasses with a pretty coating of lime zest and sea salt.

finely grated zest of 1 lime
4 tablespoons sea salt flakes
1 large bunch of fresh mint, plus extra for garnishing
500 ml/2 cups white rum
250 ml/1 cup sugar syrup
750 ml/3 cups freshly squeezed lime juice, about 12 limes (halves reserved)
500 ml/2 cups club soda or sparkling water
crushed ice, to fill

SERVES 6

Mix the lime zest and sea salt flakes, spread out on a small plate, and set aside.

Muddle the mint and rum in a large pitcher/jug by mashing the mint against the side of the pitcher with the back of a wooden spoon. Leave for 30 minutes to let the flavours mingle.

Add the sugar syrup, lime juice and club soda to the rum and stir. Add enough crushed ice to fill the pitcher/jug. Garnish with mint sprigs.

Wet the rim of a tall glass with a squeezed lime half, then dip the glass in the salt mixture and turn once. Do the same with the rest of the glasses then fill up with mojito.

Pictured on page 62.

Beergarita Granita

An excellent slushie-style drink to enjoy with brunch – tangy, refreshing and moreish.

300 g/1½ cups sugar
175 ml/⅔ cup fresh lime juice (about 6 limes)
zest of 2 limes
6 tablespoons triple sec or Cointreau
250 ml/1 cup Mexican beer (such as Corona or Sol)
8 tablespoons silver tequila

LIME SUGAR RIM
100 g/½ cup caster/superfine sugar
50 g/¼ cup sea salt

SERVES 4–6

Put 250 ml/1 cup water and the sugar in a pan over medium heat. Bring to the boil. Set aside.

Combine the lime juice, zest of 1 lime, triple sec, beer and tequila. Pour into a lipped baking sheet. Add the sugar syrup. Freeze for 1 hour, then scrape the contents with a fork once an hour until frozen into crystals.

For the lime sugar rim, combine the remaining lime zest with the sugar and salt. Dip the rims of 4–6 small glasses in water, then in the lime sugar.

Serve the granita in the sugared glasses and serve at once.

Watermelon Fizzy Punch

This drink has a natural sweetness, but the addition of cucumber and lime keeps it tasting fresh. For an alcohol-free option, just add soda water or sparkling water instead of cava.

1 small watermelon (approx. 800 g/1 lb. 12 oz.), cut into chunks, skin and seeds removed
3 small cucumbers, 1 chopped for the juice and 2 thinly sliced lengthways
1 small bunch of mint, reserving some leaves to garnish
1 pink grapefruit, ½ for juice and ½ sliced into 6 rounds
3 limes, 1 sliced in rounds and 2 juiced
30 ml/2 tablespoons light agave syrup
1 x 750-ml/25-oz. bottle of medium cava
ice cubes

SERVES 6

Put the chopped watermelon, one chopped cucumber and the mint leaves in a blender and blend together. Strain through a sieve/strainer into a jug/pitcher.

Put one slice each of grapefruit, lime and cucumber into each glass. Place the remaining sliced ingredients in the jug/pitcher and add the grapefruit juice, lime juice and agave syrup. Mix well. Top the pitcher and/or glasses with ice. Fill the pitcher with the cava and top with extra mint. Pour into tumblers to serve.

LEVANTINE

ROSÉ-ROASTED RHUBARB & PISTACHIO YOGURT POTS

SOUR-SWEET RHUBARB COMBINES PERFECTLY WITH CREAMY YOGURT, TOPPED OFF WITH PISTACHIOS AND THE PRETTIEST OF EDIBLE FLOWERS, ELEVATING SIMPLE YOGURT INTO SOMETHING QUITE ELEGANT.

400 g/14 oz. forced rhubarb
90 g/½ scant cup caster/ granulated sugar
12 cardamom pods, lightly cracked
125 ml/½ cup rosé wine
½ teaspoon freshly squeezed lemon juice
500 g/2⅓ cups thick Greek yogurt
crushed pistachios and edible flowers, to garnish

MAKES 6 SMALL SERVINGS

Cook the rhubarb the day before your brunch. Preheat the oven to 180°C (350°F) Gas 4.

Cut the rhubarb into 2.5-cm/ 1-inch pieces and toss them in a small roasting pan with the sugar, cardamom pods, wine and lemon juice. Cover securely with foil and stab half a dozen small holes in the foil.

Bake in the preheated oven for 20 minutes, until tender, then remove from the heat and leave to cool. Once cooled, decant into a sterilized jar and leave in the fridge overnight to give the cardamom and wine time to infuse the rhubarb.

When ready to assemble, divide the yogurt between 6 small serving glasses or bowls. Place a tablespoon of roasted rhubarb (removing and discarding the cardamom pods) on top of each along with another tablespoon of the liquid. Finish with pistachios and an edible flower.

BLUEBERRY, COCONUT & CHIA SEED MINI AÇAI BOWLS

A BOWL OF AÇAI IS A GREAT WAY TO KICKSTART THE DAY. PACKED WITH GOODNESS, IT HAS A CHOCOLATELY NOTE WHICH MARRIES WELL WITH THE CHIA AND COCONUT AND FEELS LIKE A TREAT.

3 small bananas
300 g/1 cup pure açai berry pulp
500 g/2⅓ cups thick Greek yogurt
3 tablespoons toasted chia seeds
6 tablespoons toasted coconut flakes
fresh blueberries and edible flowers, to garnish

MAKES 6 SMALL SERVINGS

Peel the bananas and mash the flesh with a fork, then whip it into as smooth a pulp as you can manage. Add the açai pulp and mix until thoroughly combined.

Divide the yogurt between 6 small serving bowls, then top each with a few tablespoons of the banana and açai mixture. Top with generous sprinkles of toasted chia seeds and coconut flakes and add some fresh blueberries to finish (halved if they are a little on the large side). Add an edible flower to garnish, if you like.

BUTTERNUT SQUASH WITH EGGS, CAVOLO NERO, FETA & JALAPEÑO ZHOUG

LIKE AVOCADO, BUTTERNUT SQUASH MAKES A GREAT BRUNCH ALTERNATIVE TO AVOCADO AND PROVIDES A GREAT BACKDROP FOR CONTRASTING TEXTURES, COLOURS AND FLAVOURS. IT OFFERS A SEASONAL TREAT AND A RESPITE FROM 'AVO OVERLOAD'.

500 g/1 lb. 2 oz. peeled and deseeded butternut squash, cut into 2.5-cm/1-inch chunks

1 tablespoon olive oil, plus extra for roasting the butternut squash and cavolo nero

2 small garlic cloves, crushed

1 teaspoon thyme leaves

30 g/3 tablespoons whole almonds, toasted and roughly chopped

a few sprigs of fresh mint, leaves roughly chopped

1 teaspoon pomegranate molasses

6 stems cavolo nero (approx. 70 g/2½ oz.), stalks removed, chopped into 2.5-cm/1-inch pieces

2 slices of focaccia or pitta bread

2 eggs

50 g/⅓ cup feta cheese, crumbled

1–2 tablespoons pomegranate seeds

sea salt and freshly ground black pepper

JALAPENO ZHOUG

65 g/3 cups coriander/cilantro, leaves and stalks chopped

30 g/½ cup jalapeño or green chillies/chiles, chopped

1 teaspoon sea salt

1 garlic clove, chopped

200 ml/¾ cup olive oil

20 ml/1 tablespoon plus 1 teaspoon freshly squeezed lemon juice

2 baking sheets lined with baking parchment

SERVES 2

Preheat the oven to 180°C (350°F) Gas 4.

Spread the butternut squash chunks out on a prepared baking sheet, drizzle with olive oil, season with salt and pepper and roast in the preheated oven for about 20 minutes or until tender. Remove from the oven, transfer to a bowl and mash roughly with a fork, keeping it a bit chunky.

Heat 1 tablespoon olive oil in a small pan, add the crushed garlic and thyme leaves and cook over a gentle heat for a couple of minutes. Add this to the smashed butternut squash with the chopped almonds, mint and pomegranate molasses. Season with salt and pepper.

Put the cavolo nero in a bowl, drizzle with olive oil and season with salt and pepper. Gently rub the oil into the cavolo nero with your fingers and spread it out on the second prepared baking sheet. Roast on the top shelf of the preheated oven for about 5 minutes, until crispy.

To make the Jalapeño Zhoug, put all the ingredients in a food processor and blitz to a paste.

When ready to serve, gently reheat the smashed butternut squash in a pan. Toast the focaccia or pitta bread and poach the eggs. Heap the smashed butternut squash on two plates, top with the crumbled feta, cavolo nero and pomegranate seeds. Serve with a generous dollop of Zhoug, the toasted focaccia and a poached egg.

Serve with a *Rose Martini*, recipe on page 90

SOCCA WITH CHARRED ASPARAGUS & LABNEH

SOCCA ARE DELICIOUS SAVOURY PANCAKES THAT ORIGINATE FROM NICE IN FRANCE. THEY ARE NOT AS PLIABLE AS CONVENTIONAL PANCAKES, SO BETTER TOPPED RATHER THAN FILLED AND ROLLED UP – HERE CHARRED ASPARAGUS AND LABNEH DO THE JOB NICELY.

12 fresh asparagus spears, woody ends trimmed
butter, for frying/sautéing
a pinch of chilli/hot red pepper flakes
a pinch of toasted cumin seeds
runny honey, to drizzle
leaves from a few sprigs of coriander/cilantro
lemon wedges, for squeezing
salt and freshly ground black pepper, to season

SOCCA PANCAKES
100 g/¾ cup chickpea/gram flour
½ teaspoon baking powder
a pinch of salt
leaves picked from 1 thyme sprig, or ½ teaspoon dried thyme
1 tablespoon olive oil, plus a splash for frying/sautéing

LABNEH
600 g/3 cups natural/plain yogurt (not Greek-style)
1 teaspoon salt
1 tablespoon freshly squeezed lemon juice
60 ml/¼ cup olive oil

SERVES 4

First, make the labneh. Mix the yogurt, salt and lemon juice together in a bowl. Set a sieve/strainer over a separate bowl and line it with a clean kitchen towel. Spoon in the yogurt mixture, bring the overhanging cloth together at the top and twist a few times to create a tight ball of yogurt below; you should see a little moisture starting to come through immediately. Give it a few turns to give it some pressure. Transfer to the fridge to sit for at least 12–48 hours; the longer you leave it, the thicker your labneh will be.

Before removing the labneh from the towel, squeeze it a little to remove any excess liquid then tip it out into a bowl. It can be used straightaway or, as is traditional, roll it into balls and store them in a jar submerged in olive oil; it will keep in the fridge for up to 2 weeks.

Make the pancake batter. Combine the chickpea/gram flour, baking powder, salt, thyme and 1 tablespoon of olive oil in a bowl with 225 ml/1 scant cup cold water and whisk until smooth and the consistency of single/light cream. Leave the batter to rest for at least 10 minutes at room temperature (or overnight in the fridge, to give the flour time to fully absorb the liquid).

Heat a frying pan/skillet set over a high heat and drop the asparagus spears into the hot pan, along with a small knob/pat of butter. Season generously with salt, pepper and a pinch of chilli/hot red pepper flakes. Fry/sauté for a couple of minutes over a high heat, then remove from the pan whilst still firm. Place, uncovered, in a low oven to keep warm.

Using the same frying pan/skillet, heat a splash of olive oil and once shimmering pour in about half a ladleful of batter to make a thin 20-cm/8-in. pancake. Cook for a few minutes until the pancake sets and bubbles just start to appear on its surface. Flip it over before fully cooked and cook for a further 30 seconds, before removing from the pan. Repeat until you have at least 4 pancakes, keeping them warm on a plate and covered with foil.

To assemble, put a pancake on a serving plate and smear with a few spoonfuls of labneh, top with the asparagus, a pinch of cumin seeds and a drizzle of honey, and garnish with coriander/cilantro leaves. Serve with lemon wedges for squeezing.

Serve with a *Rosé Spritzer with Rose Tea Buds*, recipe on page 89

CAULIFLOWER & CHICKPEA 'PACOS' WITH TAHINI & LIME YOGURT

MEET YOUR NEW BEST FRIEND THE 'PACO', WHERE A HAND-SIZED PANCAKE PROVIDES THE PERFECT WRAP FOR ANY FILLING. THESE PACOS ARE STUFFED WITH AN ASSORTMENT OF ZINGY MIDDLE EASTERN FLAVOURS FOR A TRENDY, TASTY BRUNCH.

225 g/1 cup ricotta cheese
3 tablespoons finely grated
  Parmesan cheese
250 ml/1 cup plus 1 tablespoon
  whole milk
1 tablespoon olive oil, plus extra
  for frying
2 eggs, separated
150 g/1 cup plus 2 tablespoons
  plain/all-purpose flour
1½ teaspoons baking powder

FILLING
350 g/12 oz. cauliflower florets
1 x 400-g/14-oz. can chickpeas,
  drained and rinsed
grated zest and juice of 1 lime
1 teaspoon ras el hanout
1 tablespoon olive oil
½ red onion, thinly sliced
½ teaspoon white sugar
2 teaspoons white wine vinegar
100 g/generous ½ cup Greek
  yogurt
1 tablespoon tahini
sea salt and freshly ground black
  pepper
pomegranate seeds, to serve
handful of fresh coriander/
  cilantro leaves, to serve

*roasting pan, lined with baking
  parchment*

MAKES 6

Preheat the oven to 190°C (375°F) Gas 5.

For the filling, cut any large cauliflower florets into bite-sized pieces and place in the prepared pan with the drained chickpeas. Combine the lime zest, ras el hanout, olive oil and a little salt and pepper in a small bowl and stir well. Add this spice paste along with 1 tablespoon of water to the cauliflower mixture and stir to evenly coat. Roast in the preheated oven for 20 minutes until the cauliflower is tender. After this, stir in 1 tablespoon lime juice and turn the oven to its lowest setting to keep the filling warm.

Meanwhile, mix the red onion slices with the sugar, ½ teaspoon salt and the vinegar and set aside for 20 minutes. Drain well and then set aside. Combine the yogurt with the tahini and remaining lime juice and season with salt and pepper. Set aside until needed.

To make the pancakes, place the ricotta, Parmesan, milk, oil and egg yolks in a bowl and whisk well, then gradually whisk in the flour and baking powder with some salt and pepper. In a separate bowl, whisk the egg whites until just stiff, then fold through the batter until evenly combined.

When ready to serve, heat a pancake pan over a medium heat and brush with oil. Pour in about 250 ml/1 cup of the batter, allowing it to spread to about 14 cm/5½ inches across. Cook for about 2 minutes until golden and then flip and cook for a further 1 minute or so until evenly golden on both sides. Remove the pancake from the pan and keep warm while you cook the remaining batter in the same way, brushing the pan with oil as needed.

To serve, in a bowl, combine the cauliflower mixture with the pickled red onion, pomegranate seeds and coriander/cilantro. Divide this mixture between the six pancakes and drizzle over the yogurt tahini sauce. Serve and eat in the same way as you would for tacos.

SMOKY AUBERGINE SHAKSHUKA

THIS SHAKSHUKA NEVER FAILS TO SATISFY THAT MID-MORNING CRAVING FOR SOMETHING A LITTLE SPICY. IF YOU DON'T HAVE A LARGE ENOUGH SKILLET, YOU CAN SIMPLY DIVIDE THE MIXTURE AND COOK IT IN TWO SMALLER PANS.

1 aubergine/eggplant
1 small onion, diced
1 garlic clove, finely sliced
1 tablespoon ras el hanout
½ teaspoon smoked paprika
1 tablespoon tomato purée/paste
1 teaspoon sugar
500 ml/2 cups passata/strained
   tomatoes
6 eggs
50 g/2 oz. feta, crumbled
a handful of fresh coriander/
   cilantro leaves, roughly chopped
   (optional)
fresh red or green chilli/chile,
   sliced
olive oil, for frying and drizzling
toasted sourdough, to serve
salt and freshly ground black
   pepper

*a 25-cm/10-in. ovenproof frying
pan/skillet*

**SERVES 3 AS A MAIN,
6 AS A SHARER**

Preheat the oven to 200°C (400°F) Gas 6.

Cut the aubergine/eggplant in half lengthways, then quarter each half to create eight full-length wedges. Fry the aubergine/eggplant wedges in a hot ovenproof frying pan/skillet with a generous glug of olive oil for 5 minutes on each side, until browned. Remove them from the pan and set aside.

Add the onion to the pan with a little more olive oil and fry for 5 minutes, then add the garlic and cook for 1 minute more. Add the ras el hanout, smoked paprika, tomato purée/paste and sugar and stir in. Follow with the passata/strained tomatoes and season well with salt and pepper. Arrange the aubergine/eggplant wedges in the sauce and leave to simmer for 5–10 minutes, then taste the sauce, adjust the seasoning to taste and remove the pan from the heat.

Make 6 small gaps in between the curled aubergine/eggplant wedges and crack the eggs, allowing a little of the white to fall away, then pour the eggs into the gaps. Sprinkle over half the feta, drizzle with olive oil and place the pan in the preheated oven for 7 minutes for medium-cooked eggs.

Remove from the oven, drizzle with a little more olive oil, scatter over the coriander/cilantro, remaining feta and chilli/chile slices and add a pinch of salt. Serve with toasted sourdough bread on the side to mop up the juices.

Pomegranate & Mint Green Tea

Green tea and ruby red jewels to replenish and refresh.

3 green teabags
2 large sprigs of fresh mint
50 ml/3½ tablespoons
   pomegranate juice
1 tablespoon pomegranate seeds
   (optional), plus a few extra
   to serve in each glass

*6-cup heatproof glass teapot
   or jug/pitcher*

SERVES 6

Place the teabags and mint in the teapot. Boil enough water to fill the teapot, let it wait for 3 minutes, then pour into the teapot and allow to infuse for up to 3 minutes. Remove the teabags from the teapot, add the pomegranate juice and seeds (if using) and serve.

Rosé Spritzer With Rose Tea Buds

Rose water has been used to add a distinctive flavour to drinks for centuries. A little goes a long way and, when combined with the rose tea buds, the subtle flavour and fragrance make this a magical drink.

1 x 750-ml/25-oz. bottle of light, crisp rosé wine
a large pinch of edible dried rose petals or rose tea buds (approx. 18 buds)
a dash of rosewater
500 ml/2 cups club soda or sparkling water
ice cubes

SERVES 6

Place a couple of ice cubes in each glass. Half-fill with rosé wine, top with 2–3 rose tea buds, a dash of rose water and top with a little soda water/club soda.

Rose Martini

A elegant twist on a classic dry martini cocktail, with indulgent white crème de cacao and fragrant rosewater. It's the perfect sipper to enjoy with a Levantine brunch.

45 ml/1⅓ oz. gin
20 ml/⅔ oz. dry vermouth
3 teaspoons white crème de cacao (optional)
3 teaspoons good-quality rose syrup or 2–3 drops rosewater
ice cubes
edible rose petals, to garnish (optional)

SERVES 1

Combine the gin, dry vermouth, crème de cacao (if using) and rose syrup or rose water in a cocktail shaker or mixing glass with a handful of ice. Stir well, then strain into a martini glass. Garnish with rose petals, if you

Lime Martini

Sharp and citrusy, this refreshing martini-style cocktail will whet your appetite and complement your Middle-Eastern inspired brunch dishes.

60 ml/2 fl oz. gin
30 ml/1 fl oz. dry vermouth
3 teaspoons triple sec
freshly squeezed juice of 1 lime
ice cubes
lime wedges, to garnish (optional)

SERVES 1

Combine the gin, vermouth, triple sec and lime juice in a cocktail shaker or mixing glass with a handful of ice cubes. Stir well, then strain into a martini glass. Garnish the drink with some lime wedges and serve at once.

NEW ORLEANS BENEDICT

BY USING A PLAIN BEIGNET INSTEAD OF AN ENGLISH MUFFIN, THIS
EGGS BENEDICT RECIPE GETS A LITTLE NEW ORLEANS FLAIR. IF THE
DOUGHNUT IS TOO MUCH, YOU CAN SUBSTITUTE WITH FRENCH
BREAD. EITHER WAY, THE TEXTURES AND TASTES COME TOGETHER
PERFECTLY TO BRING A LITTLE OF THE BAYOU TO YOUR BRUNCH.

4 eggs
4 unsugared beignets or
    unsugared doughnuts, sliced
    in half
4 Cajun-style andouille sausages,
    cooked and sliced (or other
    spicy smoked pork sausage)
2 spring onions/scallions, thinly
    sliced

CAJUN HOLLANDAISE
8 egg yolks
60 ml/¼ cup freshly squeezed
    lemon juice
1 tablespoon finely grated lemon
    zest
285 g/2½ sticks unsalted butter,
    melted
a little hot water, if needed
½ teaspoon garlic powder
½ teaspoon onion powder
½ teaspoon kosher salt
¼ teaspoon smoked paprika
¼ teaspoon celery salt
¼ teaspoon dried dill
¼ teaspoon cayenne pepper

SERVES 4

Start by making the Cajun
hollandaise. In a small saucepan
set over low heat, bring 5 cm/
2 in. of water to a bare simmer.
Place a metal bowl over the pot
to form a bain-marie.

Add the yolks, half of the lemon
juice and all of the zest to the
bowl of the bain-marie and whisk
constantly until the mixture is
thickened and ribbons form when
you pull this whisk away (this
should take about 4–5 minutes).
The yolks should double or triple
in volume.

Slowly whisk in the melted butter,
stirring constantly. If the mixture
is too thick, add a little hot water
as needed. Once the butter is fully
incorporated, stir in the second
half of lemon juice and all the
spices. Turn off the heat but keep
the mixture over the hot water to
help maintain the heat.

To poach the eggs, bring 2.5 cm/
1 in. of water to the boil in a
medium pan. Lower the heat so
that small bubbles form on the
bottom of the pan and break to
the surface only occasionally.

Crack the eggs into the water one
at a time, holding the shells close
to the water's surface and letting
the eggs slide out gently. Poach
the eggs, in two batches to keep
them from crowding, 6 minutes
for soft-cooked. Lift the eggs out
with a slotted spoon and pat dry
with a paper towel.

Arrange the halved beignets or
doughnuts on plates and carefully
place a few slices of the cooked
andouille sausage and a poached
egg on top of one half. Cover in
Cajun hollandaise, finish with
sliced spring onion/scallions and
top with the other beignet or
doughnut half. Serve immediately.

FRIED 'BALONEY' SANDWICH WITH DILL MAYO & STEAK FRIES

ALTHOUGH IT'S SPELLED 'BOLOGNA', IT'S REALLY JUST 'BALONEY' TO MANY OF US. ORIGINATING FROM BOLOGNA, ITALY, IT'S A MORTADELLA FORMED WITH PORK AND LARD (THERE ARE ALSO CHICKEN, TURKEY AND BEEF VERSIONS). WITH MULTIPLE SANDWICH FILLINGS, STEAK FRIES AND DILL MAYO, THIS MAKES A SUBSTANTIAL BRUNCH DISH.

30 g/2 tablespoons butter
4 small ciabatta rolls or brioche buns, split
12 thin slices of mortadella/bologna
2 tablespoons vegetable oil
4 eggs
4 slices of mature/sharp Cheddar cheese
2 handfuls of rocket/arugula
½ ripe tomato, thinly sliced
½ red onion, thinly sliced
green hot sauce, such as Tabasco Green Pepper Sauce, to taste (optional)

mustard, to serve (optional)
salt and freshly ground black pepper

STEAK FRIES
4 large baking potatoes, peeled
4 tablespoons olive oil
2 teaspoons paprika
2 teaspoons garlic powder
2 teaspoons chilli/chili powder
2 teaspoons onion powder

DILL MAYO
125 ml/½ cup mayonnaise
a handful of fresh chopped dill
1 tablespoon freshly squeezed lemon juice
1 teaspoon crushed/minced garlic
salt and white pepper

a heavy-based frying pan/skillet

SERVES 4

For the steak fries, preheat the oven to 230°C (450°F) Gas 8.

Cut the peeled potatoes into wedges (6–8 per potato depending on their size) and place on a baking sheet. Put all the other ingredients in a bowl and whisk with a fork to combine. Pour over the potato wedges and use your hands to toss them in the oil until well coated. Bake in the preheated oven for 45 minutes until cooked through and crisp.

Meanwhile, make up the dill mayo by combining all the ingredients in a small bowl and stirring to mix. Cover with clingfilm/plastic wrap and put in the fridge until ready to serve. Once the fries are nearly cooked, heat a medium heavy-based frying pan/skillet over a medium-high heat.

Spread butter on the cut sides of the rolls/buns and toast in the frying pan/skillet over medium heat until golden brown. Set aside. Add the mortadella/bologna slices to the frying pan/skillet and warm until slightly crisped, 2–3 minutes per side (you might have to do this in two batches). Set aside.

Add the oil to the frying pan/skillet. Crack the eggs (you may need to fry them two at a time). Fry the eggs over medium-low heat, until the egg white has set but the yolk is still soft, about 3–4 minutes. Season the eggs with salt and pepper. Place the meat on the bottom bun, followed by the egg, cheese, rocket/arugula, tomato, onions, hot sauce and mustard, if using. Spread the bottom of the top buns with 1–2 tablespoons of the dill mayo and close the sandwiches. Serve immediately with the fries and extra dill mayo for dipping.

Serve with *Whiskey Iced Tea* recipe on page 106

FISH FINGER BAPS WITH CUCUMBER & RADISH PICKLES

WE ALL FEEL NOSTALGIC FOR THIS COMFORT FOOD CLASSIC. THIS GOURMET TWIST ON THIS HUMBLE FISH FINGER/STICK SANDWICH TRANSFORMS IT INTO SOMETHING QUITE SUBLIME.

2 x 280 g/10 oz. firm white fish fillets, such as cod, haddock, pollock or hake
3 tablespoons plain/all-purpose flour
¼ teaspoon ground white pepper
½ teaspoon sea salt
1 egg, lightly beaten
40 g/1 cup panko breadcrumbs
½ teaspoon dried chilli/hot red pepper flakes
1 tablespoon freshly chopped flat-leaf parsley
1 tablespoon finely grated Parmesan cheese

vegetable oil or sunflower oil, for frying
2 tablespoons plum sauce
2 tablespoons mayonnaise
2 brioche burger buns, halved and lightly toasted
1 Little Gem/Bibb lettuce, leaves separated
2 tablespoons coriander/cilantro leaves

CUCUMBER & RADISH PICKLES
75 ml/5 tablespoons rice wine vinegar
15 g/4 teaspoons sugar
¾ teaspoon sea salt
1 cucumber, thinly sliced into discs on a mandolin
4 radishes, thinly sliced into discs on a mandolin
½ teaspoon black sesame seeds

SERVES 2

To make the pickles, combine the vinegar, sugar and salt with 2 tablespoons of water in a small saucepan and heat over a gentle heat until the sugar and salt have dissolved. Remove from the heat and add the cucumber, radishes and sesame seeds. Stir and transfer to a sealable container and set aside. This will keep in the fridge for up to 1 week.

Preheat the oven to 180°C (350°F) Gas 4.

Cut the fish fillets into fingers. Depending on the size of the fillet, you should get about four per fillet – approximately 3 x 8 cm/1¼ x 3¼ in. each.

Take three shallow dishes. Mix the flour, white pepper and salt in one, pour the beaten egg into another, and combine the breadcrumbs, chilli/hot red pepper flakes, parsley and Parmesan in the third.

Using one hand to do each step, coat the fish fingers, one by one, in the seasoned flour, then in the egg wash, shaking off any excess, and then roll in the breadcrumbs to coat. Transfer to a clean plate.

Pour 1 cm/½ in. of oil into a large frying pan/skillet and heat. To check if the oil is hot enough, put a breadcrumb into the pan and if it sizzles, it is ready. Cook the fish fingers/sticks in the hot oil until lightly brown, then turn over and brown the other side. Transfer to a lined baking sheet and place in the preheated oven for 3 minutes.

In a small bowl, combine the plum sauce with the mayonnaise and mix together. Set aside.

To assemble, put a generous spoonful of the plum mayonnaise on the top and bottom of each toasted brioche bun. Place two lettuce leaves on each bun, then the fish fingers/sticks, and top with some cucumber and radish pickle, coriander/cilantro leaves and the top of the bun.

CHICAGO STRATA

A STRATA IS A BREAKFAST OR BRUNCH 'CASSEROLE' MADE WITH MEAT, BREAD, EGGS AND HERBS. THIS STRATA IS A HOMAGE TO CHICAGO AND IT'S ESSENTIALLY A DECONSTRUCTED CHICAGO HOT DOG. USING STALE HOT DOG BUNS INSTEAD OF BREAD AND REPLACING SAUSAGE OR HAM WITH FRANKFURTERS, IT'S GREAT PAIRED WITH A SALAD OR STEAK FRIES (SEE PAGE 96).

butter, for greasing

12 eggs

250 ml/1 cup milk or single/light cream

900 g/2 lb. slightly stale hot dog buns, cut into cubes or torn into pieces

2–3 teaspoons olive oil

1 large white onion, chopped

3 dill pickle spears (or 1 large whole dill pickle), chopped

90 g/1 cup grated/shredded Cheddar cheese

4 cooked hot dogs or Polish sausages, chopped

1 x 400-g/14-oz. can chopped tomatoes, well drained, or 8–12 sundried/sunblush tomatoes, cut into pieces

23 x 33-cm/9 x 13-inch baking dish, well buttered

SERVES 4

Preheat the oven to 180°C (350°F) Gas 4. Butter the baking dish well.

Crack 7 of the eggs into a bowl and beat. Add the milk or cream and beat to combine.

Spread the hot dog bun cubes over the bottom of the buttered dish. Pour the egg and milk mixture over the bun cubes and stir to coat. Let it sit for 20 minutes for the mixture to soak into the bread. You can also soak the milk and bun cubes overnight for a lighter texture.

Meanwhile, heat the oil in a frying pan/skillet and sauté the onion until translucent. Remove from the pan and set aside. Add the pickles to the pan and sauté for about 3 minutes, until softened. Set aside.

Sprinkle half of the cheese over the soaked bun cubes. Add the sautéed onions and pickles. Add the cooked hot dogs or Polish sausage. Add the tomatoes. Layer with the remaining cheese. Beat the remaining 5 eggs and pour over the top of the strata.

Bake in the preheated oven for 45 minutes. Serve hot with a crisp leaf salad or steak fries, as preferred.

OYSTER ROCKEFELLER HASH

OYSTER ROCKEFELLER IS A DISH WHOSE ORIGINS REACH BACK AS FAR AS 1899 AND WAS NAMED AFTER THE RICHEST MAN IN THE WORLD AT THE TIME, JOHN D. ROCKEFELLER. IN ESSENCE THE DISH IS MADE UP OF OYSTERS, BUTTER, BREADCRUMBS AND HERBS. ADD IT TO POTATOES FOR A HEARTY YET DECADENT BRUNCH.

170 g/6 oz. oysters
2 slices of white sandwich bread
6 tablespoons extra virgin olive oil
¾ teaspoon anise seeds, crushed
  with a pestle and mortar
1 onion, chopped
1 fennel bulb, cored and chopped
1 kg/2 lb. Maris Piper/Yukon Gold

potatoes, peeled and cut into
  1-cm/½-inch cubes
4 garlic cloves, crushed/minced
  (about 2 teaspoons)
1–2 pinches cayenne pepper
285 g/10 oz. frozen chopped
  spinach, thawed and squeezed
  dry

4 eggs, at room temperature
salt and freshly ground black
  pepper

25-cm/10-inch cast-iron or non-stick
  frying pan/skillet

SERVES 4

Wash and drain the oysters in a sieve/strainer set over a bowl. Set aside.

Tear the bread into 6–8 pieces, then use a food processor to pulse the bread into crumbs. Continue pulsing until the crumbs are uniform with no large bits remaining.

Heat 2 tablespoons of the oil in the cast-iron or non-stick frying pan/skillet over a medium heat. Transfer the breadcrumbs to the hot oil. Sauté, stirring occasionally, until the crumbs are golden brown and crispy. Transfer to a bowl and toss with ½ teaspoon salt, ¼ teaspoon black pepper and the crushed anise seeds. Set aside.

Add 4 tablespoons olive oil to the now empty frying pan/skillet over a medium heat, and add the onion and fennel. Sauté, stirring occasionally, until the onion and fennel have softened and just started to brown, about 7–8 minutes.

While the onion and fennel are cooking, toss the potatoes with the oil, ½ teaspoon salt and ¼ teaspoon pepper in a large bowl. Pan-fry the potatoes in a separate pan for 5–7 minutes, until soft. Set aside.

Once the onion and fennel have started to brown, add the garlic, 1 teaspoon salt, ¼ teaspoon black pepper and the cayenne pepper. Stir to combine. Add the spinach, breaking it up as you add it. Add the potatoes. Stir to combine, then press into a single layer. Cook for about 3 minutes (until the potatoes start to brown), then stir, press into a single layer again and cook another 3 minutes.

Coarsely chop the oysters. Add half of them to the hash. Stir the hash again and taste for seasoning. Adjust with salt, pepper or cayenne as desired. Reduce the heat to medium low. Press the hash into a single layer a final time. Sprinkle the remaining chopped oysters evenly over the surface of the hash. Using the back of a large spoon, make 4 indents in the hash to cradle the eggs. Crack an egg into each indent and season the eggs with salt and pepper. Cover the frying pan/skillet and cook until the eggs are just set, about 5 minutes.

Divide the hash into shallow bowls, taking care not to break the yolks. Sprinkle each serving with a generous portion of the toasted breadcrumbs.

Serve with a *Caal & Dirty Martini*, recipe on page 109

PANCAKES WITH BANANA, SALTED CARAMEL & TOASTED PECANS

THESE LIGHT AND DELICATE FRENCH-STYLE PANCAKES ARE DELICIOUS STUFFED WITH AN ENDLESS VARIETY OF SWEET OR SAVOURY FILLINGS. FOR BRUNCH, IT'S HARD TO BEAT THE COMBINATION OF BITTER SWEET SALTY CARAMEL WITH BANANA AND A CRUNCH OF NUTS FOR TEXTURE.

30 g/2 tablespoons butter, plus extra melted butter for cooking
100 g/¾ cup plain/all-purpose flour
1 tablespoon caster/granulated sugar
a pinch of salt
1 egg plus 1 egg yolk
350 ml/scant 1½ cups milk

SALTED CARAMEL SAUCE
200 g/1 cup caster/granulated sugar
90 g/6 tablespoons butter
½ teaspoon sea salt flakes, plus extra to serve
120 ml/½ cup single/light cream

FILLING
2 bananas, peeled and sliced
100 g/¾ cup toasted pecans, crushed

SERVES 6

To make the pancakes, melt the 30 g/2 tablespoons butter in a small saucepan and set aside.

Sift the flour into a large bowl and add the sugar and a pinch of salt. In a separate bowl, lightly beat the egg and egg yolk and stir together with the milk and the cooled melted butter. Pour this mixture into the flour and whisk together until smooth.

Heat a small frying pan/skillet over a medium heat and brush with extra melted butter. Using a small ladle or a 125-ml/½-cup measuring cup, pour some batter into the pan, swirling the batter around the pan so it just covers the base. Cook for a minute or so, until the edges of the pancake begin to brown and the underside is golden. Slide a spatula underneath and gently flip the pancake over to cook on the other side for 30 seconds. Lift it out and set aside on a plate. Repeat the process until all the batter is used up. Cover the pancakes with foil to keep them warm.

To make the sauce, melt the sugar in a small pan over a medium heat, stirring continuously with a rubber spatula (don't use metal or the sugar may crystallize). Once the sugar has liquefied and turned a rich caramel colour, remove from the heat and add the butter and salt, mixing until well incorporated. Place the saucepan back on a low heat and pour in the cream. It will bubble up. Beat it well until it's glossy and smooth (about 30 seconds) and then take it off the heat.

To assemble the pancakes, put a few slices of banana and some crushed toasted pecans on each pancake and then fold into a triangle and drizzle well with the sauce. Sprinkle with extra sea salt and serve.

Whiskey Iced Tea

With the smokiness of the whiskey, the tart sweetness of the peaches and aromatic vanilla, which enhances all the other flavours, this iced tea is a real winner.

1 litre/4¼ cups water
6 peach-flavoured teabags
½ teaspoon vanilla extract
1–2 tablespoons agave, to taste
100 ml/⅓ cup peach juice/nectar
150–200 ml/⅔–scant 1 cup
    whiskey (depending how strong
    you like it)
ice cubes

SCORCHED PEACHES
3 peaches, stoned/pitted and
    quartered
1 tablespoon runny honey
1 teaspoon light brown sugar
a pinch of vanilla powder
    (optional)

SERVES 6

Bring the water to the boil in a small saucepan. Remove the pan from the heat and add the teabags and vanilla and let steep for 5 minutes. Remove the teabags and stir in the agave until dissolved. Transfer to a large jug/pitcher, add the peach nectar and stir to combine. Chill in the fridge for at least 1 hour. Add the whiskey to the jug/pitcher and pour into ice-filled glasses.

To scorch the peaches, place them on a baking sheet, drizzle with honey, top with sugar and grill/broil under a very hot grill/broiler until scorched. Serve in each glass, with extra on the side for people to nibble on. Top with a pinch of vanilla powder and serve.

Rosé, Bourbon & Blue

Prepare to be blown away by this moreish julep-style punch. The puréed blueberries give the drink its distinctive flavour and juicy body, while the tannin is just detectable underneath the smoky notes of the bourbon.

8 tablespoons raw cane sugar
250 g/2 cups fresh blueberries, rinsed and picked over for stems
500 ml/2 cups brewed unsweetened black tea, cooled
330 ml/1⅓ cups dark pink fruity rosé wine
250 ml/1 cup bourbon
175 ml/¾ cup freshly squeezed lemon juice
lemon slices and blueberries, to garnish
ice cubes

SERVES 6–8

Stir the sugar with 7 tablespoons of hot water in a small bowl until the sugar is dissolved. Transfer to the cup of a blender. Add 65 g/½ cup blueberries and purée. Set a sieve/strainer over a large jug/pitcher. Strain the blueberry mixture, pressing on the solids with the back of a wooden spoon to extract as much liquid as possible. Discard the solids. Add the cooled tea, rosé, bourbon and lemon juice to the jug/pitcher. Cover and refrigerate until chilled, about 2 hours.

When ready to serve, add the remaining blueberries to the jug/pitcher, fill old-fashioned glasses with ice cubes and divide the drink among the glasses. Garnish each serving with a lemon slice and a blueberry. Serve at once.

Pictured opposite.

Cool & Dirty Martini

A deliciously briny martini with the addition of cooling cucumber – lip-smackingly good!

½ cucumber, chopped
60 ml/2 oz. gin
30 ml/1 oz. dry vermouth
1–2 teaspoons olive brine
ice cubes
cucumber flower or green olive, to garnish (optional)

SERVES 1

Muddle the cucumber in the base of a cocktail shaker or mixing glass, then add the gin, dry vermouth and olive brine with a handful of ice cubes. Stir well, then strain into a martini glass. Garnish with a cucumber flower or olive, if you like, and serve immediately.

Pictured on pages 91 and 103.

ASIAN-STYLE

COCONUT CHIA PUDDING POTS WITH MANGO & MINT

THESE LITTLE POTS ARE DECEPTIVELY DECADENT AND DELICIOUS DESPITE CONTAINING NO DAIRY OR REFINED SUGAR. THEY'RE A LIGHTER AND HEALTHIER ALTERNATIVE TO YOUR TRADITIONAL OAT-BASED BRUNCH DISHES. REMEMBER TO START THIS RECIPE IN ADVANCE OF YOUR BRUNCH.

1 ripe mango, peeled, stoned/
   pitted and finely diced
2 teaspoons ginger syrup
finely chopped leaves from
   4 sprigs of fresh mint
coconut yogurt, to serve
seeds from ½ pomegranate,
   to serve

CHIA PUDDING MIX
400 ml/1⅔ cups coconut milk
1 tablespoon clear honey
4 cardamom pods, lightly bruised
1 teaspoon vanilla extract
165 g/1 cup chia seeds

SERVES 4

To make the chia pudding mix, put the coconut milk, honey, cardamom pods and vanilla into a saucepan and heat until it just reaches the boil. Remove from the heat and leave to infuse for at least 20 minutes, or until cool.

Strain the mixture into a large bowl and discard the cardamom pods. Stir in the chia seeds and whisk for 1–2 minutes, making sure the chia seeds don't clump together. Cover with clingfilm/plastic wrap and leave overnight or for a minimum of 4 hours in the fridge. The chia seeds will swell so make sure your bowl has plenty of room.

Put the mango flesh into a bowl with the ginger syrup. Add the chopped mint and gently combine.

To serve, spoon the chia pudding mix into 4 serving glasses and top each with a dollop of coconut yogurt, the mango and mint, and a few pomegranate seeds.

SPICY PORK BURGERS WITH MANGO SALSA & FENNEL SLAW

THE SPICY ASIAN FLAVOURS AND SWEET FRESH MANGO SALSA SET THIS SUCCULENT PORK BURGER APART FROM A TRADITIONAL BEEF BURGER, AND MAKES A LIGHTER BRUNCH ALTERNATIVE TOO.

3 tablespoons olive oil
115 g/¾ cup finely diced onion
3 garlic cloves, crushed
a 4-cm/1½-inch piece of fresh ginger, peeled and finely grated
900 g/2 lb. minced/ground pork
2 long red chillies/chiles, deseeded and finely chopped
1 tablespoon fish sauce
2 tablespoons freshly chopped coriander/cilantro
60 g/2¼ oz. streaky bacon, chopped
2 eggs
sea salt and freshly ground black pepper

MANGO SALSA
2 mangoes, peeled, pitted and very finely diced
1 long red chilli/chile, deseeded and finely diced
1 tablespoon freshly chopped coriander/cilantro
1 tablespoon roughly chopped mint leaves
½ medium red onion, finely diced
freshly squeezed juice of 1 lime
2 teaspoons palm sugar/jaggery

FENNEL SLAW
2 heaped tablespoons mayonnaise
grated zest and freshly squeezed juice of 1 lemon
200 g/7 oz. (about 1 small) fennel bulb, trimmed, sliced into rings
a bunch of freshly chopped mint
40 g/scant 1 cup freshly chopped flat-leaf parsley
40 g/1½ oz. rocket/arugula
½ red onion, thinly sliced

TO SERVE
6 burger buns
mayonnaise

SERVES 6

To make the salsa, mix all of the ingredients together in a bowl and set aside.

To make the slaw, mix the mayonnaise with the lemon zest and juice and then dress the fennel straight away to prevent the fennel discolouring. Gently mix through the herbs, rocket/arugula and red onion. Set aside.

For the burgers, heat 1 tablespoon of the oil in a frying pan/skillet and sauté the onion, garlic and ginger over a gentle heat until soft. Remove from the heat and allow to cool.

Place all the remaining ingredients in a large bowl, add the onion mixture and combine. Season with salt and pepper. Form the burger mixture into 6 burger patties. Refrigerate until ready to cook.

Preheat the oven to 170°C (325°F) Gas 3.

Heat the remaining 2 tablespoons of oil in a large frying pan/skillet over a medium heat and fry the burger patties for 4 minutes, turning once, until brown on both sides. You may need to do this in batches, depending on the size of your pan/skillet. Transfer the burgers to a baking sheet and finish them off in the preheated oven for a further 10 minutes.

While the burgers are cooking, halve, then lightly toast the burger buns under the grill/broiler. Spread some mayonnaise on the bottom buns and top with the pork burgers, salsa and the other halves of the buns. Serve with the fennel slaw on the side.

Serve with a *Lime, Cucumber & Lychee Gin & Tonic*, recipe on page 120

MOONG DAL PANCAKES WITH PORK

**THESE SAVOURY KOREAN PANCAKES OFTEN CONTAIN KIMCHI, THE
SPICED PICKLED CABBAGE, BUT THIS VERSION USES GREEN BEANS
INSTEAD. EITHER WAY, THEY MAKE A DELICIOUS BRUNCHTIME
SNACK. REMEMBER TO SOAK THE DAL OVERNIGHT.**

400 g/2 cups dried moong dal
   (skinned and split mung beans),
   soaked overnight
2 tablespoons soy sauce, plus
   extra to serve
3 garlic cloves, crushed
1 tablespoon grated fresh ginger
4 tablespoons vegetable oil
250 g/8 oz. minced/ground lean
   pork
1 leek, trimmed and finely
   chopped
125 g/4 oz. green beans, fresh or
   frozen, chopped into small
   pieces
chopped pickled cucumber and
   sliced red chilli/chile (optional),
   to serve

MAKES ABOUT 12

Drain the moong dal and put them in the food processor. Blend them
finely, then add 400 ml/1⅔ cups of water, the soy sauce, all but
1 crushed garlic clove and all but ½ teaspoon of the grated ginger.
Process the mixture to a smooth purée. Transfer the moong dal purée
to a bowl, then leave the batter to sit for at least 30 minutes.

Heat 2 tablespoons of the oil in a frying pan/skillet or wok and fry the
remaining garlic for 1 minute before adding the pork, together with the
remaining ½ teaspoon of grated ginger and salt. Stir well and continue
to cook until the pork is cooked through, then add the chopped leek
and green beans and continue to cook gently until the vegetables are
half-cooked, but not soft. Take off the heat and set aside to cool.

Fold the cooled pork mixture into the pancake batter. Heat a teaspoon
of oil in a non-stick frying pan/skillet over a medium heat, and when it
is hot, pour a spoonful of the batter into the pan/skillet. Spread out the
batter with the back of the ladle until it forms an 8-cm/3-inch circle.
Repeat the process with more batter, frying several pancakes at a time.

Cook the pancakes until golden brown on the underside and until tiny
holes have begun to appear on the upper surface, then flip them over
and cook the other side. This will probably take around 5 minutes on
each side. It is important not to overheat the pan and burn the surface
before the inside is cooked, but it must be hot enough for the pancakes
to brown and crisp.

Keep warm while you make the other pancakes in the same way,
brushing the frying pan/skillet or wok with oil before cooking each
batch. Serve straight away with a bowl of soy sauce for dipping, and
pickled cucumber and some sliced red chilli/chile, if desired.

Serve with Mango Pepper Baba, recipe on page 123

BANANA FRITTERS

THESE VIETNAMESE-STYLE HOT, MELTY BANANAS FRIED IN A COCONUT-RICE-FLOUR BATTER ARE THE ULTIMATE BRUNCHTIME TREAT WHEN YOU CRAVE SOMETHING SWEET. FOR THIS RECIPE, JUST-RIPE BANANAS WORK BEST.

6 just-ripe bananas
200 g/1½ cups rice flour
400 ml/1¾ cups coconut milk
100 g/½ cup caster/granulated
    sugar
dash of vanilla extract or seeds
    from 1 vanilla bean/pod
4 tablespoons sunflower oil
icing/confectioners' sugar, to dust

COCONUT CUSTARD
400 ml/¼ cups coconut milk
1 teaspoon salt
1 teaspoon sugar

SERVES 6–10

Cut the bananas in half lengthways, then chop them into 7.5-cm/3-in. pieces. Set aside.

Mix together the rice flour, coconut milk, sugar and vanilla in a bowl, making sure it is smooth and free of lumps. Add the bananas and mix to coat in the batter.

Heat the oil in a frying pan/skillet over a medium heat and fry the bananas, in batches, for 2–3 minutes on each side or until golden brown. Set aside on paper towels.

To make the coconut custard, put the coconut milk, salt and sugar in a saucepan over a low heat and heat until warm.

Dust the fritters with icing/confectioners' sugar and serve warm or at room temperature with the warm coconut custard for pouring.

Lime, Cucumber & Lychee Gin & Tonic

The combination of lime, cucumber and lychee is just magical – light, fresh, floral and with a gentle sweetness. A perfect match for Asian-style flavours.

200 ml/scant 1 cup lychee juice
200 ml/scant 1 cup gin
½ cucumber, cut into thick slices
1 can lychees in syrup, drained
3 sprigs of mint, leaves picked
2 limes, sliced
ice cubes

SERVES 6

Mix the lychee juice and gin in a jug/pitcher and add some ice. Thread a piece of cucumber and a lychee onto 6 cocktail sticks/toothpicks and set aside.

Place some ice into the glasses, pour over the gin mixture, garnish with lime slices and mint leaves and top with a lychee and cucumber cocktail stick/toothpick.

Pictured right and on page 114

Jasmine Blossom

The beautiful floral perfume of jasmine tea, given a little backbone by a dash of gin and the almond scent of orgeat, makes this an unusual but delightful daytime cocktail that will intrigue your guests.

35 ml/1½ oz freshly brewed
    strong jasmine tea, chilled
5 ml/1 teaspoon orgeat syrup
10 ml/⅓ oz gin
 well-chilled Asti Spumante or
    other semi-sweet sparkling
    wine, to top
jasmine leaves or blossoms,
    to garnish (optional)

SERVES 1

Pour the jasmine tea, orgeat syrup and gin into an ice-filled cocktail shaker and shake well. Strain into a chilled Champagne flute or small coupe and top with Asti. Garnish with jasmine, if you like, and serve.

Hibiscus Iced Tea

A refreshing and tart iced tea that can be made with teabags if you can't find dried hibiscus flowers.

HIBISCUS SYRUP
3 tablespoons edible dried
   hibiscus flowers
25 ml/1½ tablespoons sugar
   syrup

TO SERVE
soda water or sparkling water
ice cubes
mint sprigs
orange slices, halved

SERVES 4

To make the hibiscus syrup, bring 1 litre/4 cups of water to the boil in a saucepan. Remove from the heat and allow to cool for 5 minutes. Add the hibiscus flowers and allow to steep for 1 hour. Strain into a large jug/pitcher and add the sugar syrup.

Refrigerate for at least an hour before serving.

Serve in a tall glass with ice cubes, diluted with soda water or sparkling water to taste, and garnished with a sprig of mint and halved slices of orange.

Note: Unused hibiscus syrup can be stored in a sealed glass jar and will keep in the fridge for a few days.

Mango Pepper Boba

Boba (bubble tea) is a sweet Taiwanese drink made with large tapioca pearls. It comes in a kaleidoscope of colours and flavours. This is to be sipped slowly on a hot day, without getting the pearls stuck in your straw! Wide straws are best.

¼ cup/60 ml sugar syrup
6 makrut lime leaves
2 cups/340 g chopped mango,
   fresh or frozen
2 cups/350 g ice chips/crushed ice
1 teaspoon Lampong peppercorns
1 cup/75 g cooked boba pearls
   (large tapioca balls)

SERVES 4

Heat the syrup in a small pan, add the makrut lime leaves, then remove from the heat and set aside to cool.

Place the cooled, strained lime leaf-infused syrup, mango, ice chips/crushed ice and peppercorns in a blender and process until smooth. Divide the pearls between the glasses, then top with the mango juice.

Add a wide straw to each drink and serve.

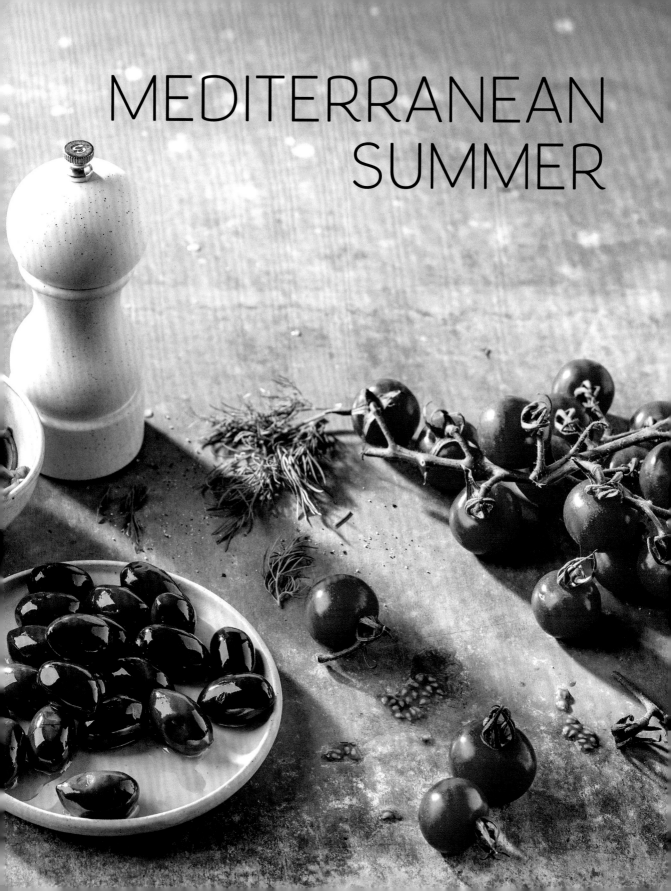

MEDITERRANEAN SUMMER

SPANISH-STYLE TORTILLA WITH FRESH TOMATO SALSA

THE COMBINATION OF EGGS, POTATOES AND ONIONS CREATES A BRUNCH DISH THAT IS MORE THAN THE SUM OF ITS PARTS. WHATEVER YOU DO, DON'T OVERCOOK THE TORTILLA – YOU WANT A SLIGHT WOBBLE.

250 ml/1 cup olive oil
1 white or red onion, sliced
350 g/12 oz. waxy potatoes, peeled, halved and sliced
5 eggs
60 g/⅔ cup grated/shredded strong/sharp Cheddar cheese
80 g/½ cup smoked bacon lardons/cubed thick-cut smoked bacon
¼ green (bell) pepper, deseeded and diced
salt and freshly ground black pepper

FRESH TOMATO SALSA
150 g/5½ oz. baby plum tomatoes, diced
1 tablespoon finely diced red onion
½ fresh green chilli/chile, deseeded and diced
2 tablespoons chopped flat-leaf parsley
3 tablespoons olive oil
1 tablespoon cider vinegar

a 20-cm/8-inch non-stick, deep frying pan/skillet

SERVES 4

To make the salsa, combine all the ingredients in a small bowl, season generously with salt and pepper, cover and set aside.

Add the oil and onion to a frying pan/skillet set over a medium heat and sauté for about 6–8 minutes, or until the onion starts to caramelize, then add the potatoes and continue cooking for about 10–15 minutes more, until the potatoes soften.

Meanwhile, crack the eggs into a mixing bowl, season generously with salt and pepper and break them up with a fork (there is no need to whisk them), then tip in the grated cheese.

Use a slotted spoon to remove the cooked onion and potatoes from the pan (leaving the oil behind) and fold them into the egg mixture. Cover the bowl and let the mixture steep for 15 minutes, after which time the mixture will have thickened as the potatoes soak up moisture from the eggs.

Put the pan back over the heat and sauté the lardons for a few minutes before adding the (bell) pepper. When the lardons have turned golden, add them and the pepper to the bowl with the eggs. Wipe the pan with paper towels, leaving a little residual oil.

Heat up the pan again and once it's hot, pour in the egg mixture – it will fill most of the pan. Cook over a medium-high heat for about 4–5 minutes, until the tortilla is just pulling away from the edge of the pan (it will still be runny in the centre). Lay a plate larger than the pan over the tortilla, hold it firmly, then confidently flip it over so the tortilla is now resting on the plate and the pan is upside-down on top.

Put the pan back on the heat and gently slide the tortilla off the plate and back into the pan. Continue cooking for just a couple of minutes, then place a clean plate back on top of the pan again and flip it out. Leave to rest for a few minutes before serving.

Strain the salsa and discard the excess liquid. Spoon it in a little pile in the centre of your tortilla and serve.

OUZO-CURED SALMON BAGELS

HOMECURING IS REALLY SO EASY – A FEW DAYS IN THE FRIDGE, YES, BUT THE PREPARATION IS QUICK. THIS SALMON IS GREAT TO HAVE ON STANDBY FOR IMPROMPTU BRUNCHES. SLICE IT INTO PIECES AND EAT WITH TOASTED BAGELS WITH A CREAM CHEESE AND HORSERADISH WHIP.

200 g/1 cup white granulated sugar
100 g/½ cup demerara sugar
400 g/2 cups coarse sea salt
1 side of fresh salmon (about 1 kg/2 lb. 4 oz.), deboned, skin on
60 ml/¼ cup ouzo
a small handful of freshly chopped dill

plain bagels, lightly toasted, to serve
large caper berries and dill flowers, to serve

SPICE MIX
2 star anise
12 cloves
1 tablespoon fennel seeds
1 tablespoon coriander seeds
4 bay leaves

CREAM CHEESE & HORSERADISH WHIP
4 tablespoons cream cheese
4 tablespoons horseradish sauce
a little freshly squeezed lemon juice
freshly ground black pepper

SERVES 12

Grind up the spice mix ingredients using a pestle and mortar. Combine this mix with both the sugars and salt – this is the dry curing mixture.

Take a large roasting pan (with high sides and big enough to take the salmon laid out flat) and sprinkle about a quarter of the dry curing mixture over the base of it, roughly where the fish will lay. Lay the salmon, skin-side down, in the pan and pour over the ouzo, massaging it into the flesh with your fingers.

Sprinkle the rest of the dry curing mixture over the fish, trying to completely cover the top and sides and pat it down. Take a sheet of clingfilm/plastic wrap and place over the fish, tucking it in around the edges as much as possible, then cover the fish again with another sheet of clingfilm/plastic wrap.

Place a small chopping board or baking sheet on top of the fish, ensuring the edges of it fit inside the roasting pan. Pop the whole thing in the fridge, weighing down with a few heavy food cans.

Leave in the fridge for a minimum of 2 days, ideally 3. Once a day, pour away the juices (no need to remove all the clingfilm/plastic wrap, just open a gap in one corner to pour the liquid away whilst holding the fish in place).

After a few days, remove the fish from the pan, wiping away as much of the curing mixture from the fish as possible. The fish should be nice and firm by now. Rinse the fish under cold water to remove all traces of the cure.

Pat dry with paper towels and cover the flesh side of the salmon with finely chopped dill and pat it down to help it stick. Carve thin slices of the salmon, starting at the tail end and carving at an angle towards the tail.

Mix the cream cheese and horseradish together with a few drops of lemon juice and a few grinds of black pepper to make a tasty whip.

When ready to serve, lightly toast some sliced bagels, spread a dollop of the cream cheese and horseradish whip over each side and top with a couple of slithers of the salmon. Garnish with large caper berries and dill flowers.

Any remaining salmon can be stored in the fridge wrapped in baking parchment for up to 5 days (it's best to carve the salmon to stop it drying out).

Serve with Elderflower Sparkle, recipe on page 138

MEDITERRANEAN ROSTI WITH GREEN TOMATO SOFRITO

THESE FRESH AND SHARP-TASTING COURGETTE/ZUCCHINI, POTATO AND FETA CHEESE ROSTI ARE FRIED UNTIL CRISP AND THEN TOPPED WITH AN EGG AND A TANGY GREEN TOMATO SOFRITO SAUCE. MAKE MORE SOFRITO THAN YOU THINK YOU NEED AS IT IS SO VERY MOREISH!

100 g/3½ oz. floury potatoes,
  unpeeled but well scrubbed
50 g/2 oz. courgette/zucchini
1 red or white onion, thinly sliced
40 g/1½ oz. feta cheese, crumbled
a generous pinch of dried mint or
  leaves from 3 sprigs of mint,
  finely chopped
2 tablespoons olive oil
a splash of white wine vinegar,
  for poaching the eggs
salt and freshly ground black
  pepper

GREEN TOMATO SOFRITO
about 2 tablespoons olive oil
1 red onion, finely diced
½ green (bell) pepper, deseeded
  and finely diced
1 garlic clove, crushed
1 fresh green chilli/chile, diced
3 large green tomatoes, deseeded
  and flesh chopped
6 sprigs of flat-leaf parsley,
  chopped
6 sprigs of coriander/cilantro,
  chopped

SERVES 2

To make the sofrito, add a splash of olive oil to a large frying pan/skillet and add the onion, (bell) pepper, garlic and chilli/chile. Sauté very gently over a low heat for about 10 minutes, until softened and starting to caramelize. Season with salt and pepper.

Add the green tomatoes, parsley and coriander/cilantro (including the stalks) and simmer for another 20 minutes over a low heat, or until the sauce has thickened – add a splash of water if it starts to catch. Once cooked, fold in a little more olive oil to give it a silky finish, cover and set aside until ready to use.

Grate the potatoes (using the side of your box grater with the largest holes), then use your hands to squeeze out the excess liquid from the potatoes. Put in a mixing bowl. Grate the courgette/zucchini in the same way and again squeeze the excess liquid out. Add to the bowl with the grated potato. Fold in the sliced onion, feta cheese and mint. This should be quite a dry mixture.

Heat the olive oil in a non-stick frying pan/skillet set over a high heat. Grab a quarter of the rosti mixture and use your hands to form it into a tight ball, then flatten to about 2 cm/¾ inch thick and put into the hot oil. Repeat to make 4 rostis. The secret to success here is not to touch the rostis while they are cooking as you need a strong crust to form and hold it all together. After about 5 minutes use a fish slice to gently flip them over and cook for a further 5 minutes, again without disturbing them.

Remove the rostis from the pan and divide between serving plates. Spoon the sofrito generously over the top and serve.

PANCETTA & EGG BRUNCH TART WITH TOMATO CHUTNEY

WHEN CONSTRUCTING THIS TART, IT IS IMPORTANT TO CREATE A GOOD WELL FOR THE EGG TO SIT IN TO PREVENT ANY SPILLAGES. WHEN YOU ARRANGE THE FIRST LAYER OF LEEKS, CREATE THE WELLS AND REINFORCE THEM WITH THE PANCETTA – SERIOUS BUILDING SKILLS ARE REQUIRED HERE!

50 g/3½ tablespoons butter, roughly chopped
1 leek, thinly sliced
1 garlic clove, finely chopped
2 tablespoons roughly chopped thyme and oregano (or 1 teaspoon each of dried thyme and oregano)
8 filo/phyllo pastry sheets
10 slices pancetta
6 eggs, at room temperature
1 tablespoon olive oil
1½ handfuls of rocket/arugula, coarsely chopped

ROASTED CHERRY TOMATO CHUTNEY
500 g/3 cups cherry tomatoes, halved
1 red onion, finely chopped
2 garlic cloves, crushed
50 ml/3½ tablespoons apple cider vinegar
1 teaspoon white mustard seeds
2 tablespoons brown sugar
½ teaspoon chilli/hot red pepper flakes
a pinch of dried curry leaves
1 bay leaf
sea salt
2 tablespoons olive oil

20 x 29-cm/8 x 11-inch baking sheet

SERVES 4–6

Preheat the oven to 180°C (350°F) Gas 4.

To make the chutney, place all the ingredients in a shallow baking pan, drizzle with the oil, cover and roast in the preheated oven for 50 minutes until they are soft, tossing occasionally to avoid sticking. Uncover the pan, increase the temperature to 200°C (400°F) Gas 6 and return to the oven to caramelize for approx. 10–15 minutes. Leave to cool.

To make the tart, melt half the butter in a large frying pan/skillet over a medium heat, add the leek and garlic and stir occasionally until starting to caramelize (approx. 6–7 minutes). Add the herbs to the pan and set aside off the heat.

Melt the remaining butter and brush the base and sides of the baking sheet. Trim the filo/phyllo pastry sheets to fit the inside the baking sheet. Place the first pastry sheet on the baking sheet, brush with butter, then lay over another pastry sheet and repeat until all the pastry is used.

Spread the leek mixture over the pastry base. Make six evenly spaced indentations in the leek mixture. Place the pancetta over the tart, leaving the indentations free for the eggs. Place in the preheated oven for 7 minutes.

Crack the eggs into the indentations, drizzle with oil and bake until the tart is set and the eggs are medium cooked (approx. 10–15 minutes). Scatter over the rocket/arugula and return to the oven until just wilted. Serve with the roasted cherry tomato chutney.

Serve with Apricot & Basil Mimosas, recipe on page 140

FENNEL & GREEN APPLE SALAD

THIS IS A REFRESHING SALAD THAT WORKS REALLY WELL AS A BRUNCH SIDE DISH. THE FENNEL AND TARRAGON BRING A NOTE OF ANISEED AND THE APPLES ADD A CRISP SHARPNESS. SERVE THIS CHILLED, STRAIGHT FROM THE FRIDGE.

1 fennel bulb
freshly squeezed juice of 1 lime
1 tart, crisp green eating apple,
  such as a Granny Smith
¼ cucumber
½ fresh green chilli/chile
  (optional)
a small handful of fresh mint
  leaves
leaves from a sprig of fresh
  tarragon
1 tablespoon olive oil
a pinch of salt

SERVES 4

Thinly slice the fennel bulb and chop the fronds. Put it in a large bowl and pour over the freshly squeezed lime juice.

Leave the peel on the apple. Core it, slice in half and cut into thin slices about 3 mm/⅛ inch thick. Add to the fennel in the bowl and toss everything in the lime juice as it will help to prevent the apple slices from browning.

Quarter the cucumber lengthways, then use a spoon to scoop out the watery seeds. Thinly slice the cucumber to about the same thickness as the apple and add it to the bowl with the fennel and apple.

Deseed the green chilli/chile (if using), slice very thinly and add to the bowl. Finally, rip the mint and tarragon straight into the bowl (go easy on the tarragon as it does have quite a strong flavour).

Drizzle over the olive oil and add the pinch of salt. Toss everything together once last time and chill in the fridge until ready to serve, but try to prepare it no more than 30 minutes before serving, to keep everything nice and crisp.

CITRUS SALAD
WITH ROSEWATER CARAMEL

THIS IS ANOTHER BEAUTIFUL SIDE DISH FOR A SUMMERY BRUNCH – COLOURFUL SLICES OF CITRUS FRUITS DRENCHED IN A FRAGRANT ROSEWATER CARAMEL SYRUP AND TOPPED WITH CRUNCHY PISTACHIOS AND DARK CHOCOLATE SHAVINGS. THE RED GRAPEFRUIT ADDS A BITTER SHARPNESS, BUT YOU CAN LEAVE IT OUT, IF PREFERRED.

2 blood oranges
2 oranges
1 red or pink grapefruit (optional)
2 kiwi fruit, gold if you can find these
12 small fresh mint leaves
40 g/⅓ cup pistachio nuts, lightly crushed
1 tablespoon dried edible rose petals, lightly crushed
a 40-g/1½-oz. bar of dark/bittersweet chocolate, chilled
thick Greek yogurt, to serve

ROSEWATER CARAMEL SYRUP
150 ml/⅔ cup warm water
200 g/1 cup caster/superfine sugar
1 cinnamon stick
30 g/2 tablespoons butter
a small pinch of salt
1 tablespoon rosewater

SERVES 6

Top and tail all the fruit and then hold each piece, one of the cut-sides down, on a flat surface and use a sharp knife to slice away all the peel and pith (or kiwi skin) from the outside to reveal the flesh. Turn each piece on its side and cut the fruit into thin (just under 5-mm/¼-in.) slices. Arrange the slices on a large, flat platter.

To make the rosewater syrup, put half the warm water in a small saucepan with the sugar and cinnamon stick and set over a very low heat. Stir gently until the sugar has dissolved, then turn up the heat and stop stirring (you don't want it to start to crystallizing). Swirl the pan as it turns a blonde colour and starts to caramelize (this will take about 5 minutes), at which point take the pan off the heat and beat in the butter, rapidly followed by the remaining water. Keep beating until both are fully incorporated, then add the salt and return the pan to a very low heat. Bring to a simmer for 2 minutes, remove from the heat and once it's stopped bubbling, stir in the rosewater. Discard the cinnamon stick.

Pour the warm syrup over the prepared fruit platter, scatter over the mint leaves, pistachios and rose petals and use a vegetable peeler to shave a little chocolate over the top. Serve with Greek yogurt on the side (or add a few dollops to the platter before garnishing).

Summer Sangria

There isn't really a definitive recipe for sangria as you can add any kind of seasonal fruit and top with wine and a splash of brandy. You can substitute a low or no-alcohol wine too. In summer, lighter bright wines, such as rosé, are best used. Night-time sangrias, however, can use bolder reds.

1 yellow peach
1 white peach
2 plums
1 orange, unpeeled
12 strawberries
½ cup/50 g blueberries
2 x 750-ml/25-oz. bottles of rosé wine
120 ml/½ cup brandy
60 ml/4 tablespoons sugar syrup
crushed ice

SERVES 6–8

Cut the peaches and plums in half, remove the stones/pits, and chop the fruit into 2.5-cm/1-inch chunks. Cut the orange into 2.5-cm/1-inch chunks. Slice the strawberries and place all the cut fruit, along with the blueberries, in a large pitcher and fill with crushed ice.

Pour in the rosé, brandy and simple syrup and stir. Cover and refrigerate until ready to serve.

Elderflower Sparkle

Add some sparkle to your summer's day with this light refreshing drink. Adding the gold leaf brings a touch of bling to start your day.

20 ml/4 teaspoons elderflower liqueur
120 ml/½ cup vodka
1 lemon, sliced
soda water/club soda
ice cubes
gold leaf (optional)

SERVES 4–6

Fill a large jug/pitcher with ice and pour in the liqueur, vodka, sliced lemon and soda water/club soda. Top each glass with gold leaf and serve.

Pictured opposite and on page 139.

Apricot & Basil Mimosas

This is a wonderful brunch drink – light and fizzy with herbal aromatics from the basil. Make the apricot and basil purée ahead of time (store it in the fridge for up to 24 hours) and when guests arrive all you have to do is add chilled Champagne.

120 ml/½ cup sugar syrup
4 basil leaves
8 very ripe apricots, stoned/pitted
1 x 750-ml/25-oz. bottle of
   Champagne, chilled

SERVES 4

In a small saucepan bring the simple syrup and basil to the boil over a medium-high heat. Remove the pan from the heat and let the syrup cool, allowing the basil to infuse. When cold, remove the basil. Place the apricots and cooled simple syrup in a blender and process until smooth.

To make the mimosas, pour the apricot purée a quarter of the way up a chilled Champagne flute. Top up with the chilled Champagne and serve.

Pictured on page 140.

Just Peachy Punch

A pale pink Provençal rosé, peach purée and French brandy enjoy a ménage à trois here with delicious results.

4 ripe peaches, stoned/pitted and
   cut into wedges
75 ml/2½ oz. French brandy
75 ml/2½ oz. peach schnapps
1 x 750-ml/25-oz. bottle of light,
   crisp rosé, well chilled
375 ml/1½ cups bottled French
   peach juice/nectar or purée
   (see note)
1–1½ litres/4–6 cups Indian tonic
   water, well-chilled
peach slices and fresh basil
   sprigs, to garnish
ice cubes

SERVES 6–8

Put the peaches in a large jug/pitcher, pour over the brandy and schnapps and leave to marinate for a few hours.

When ready to serve, pour the wine into the jug/pitcher along with the peach juice/nectar and add plenty of ice cubes. Stir and top up to taste with tonic. Pour into ice-cube-filled tumblers, garnish each serving with a peach slice and a sprig of basil and serve at once.

NOTE: If you can't find bottled peach juice or purée, blend about 6 stoned/pitted ripe peaches (to yield 375 ml/1½ cups of juice) and pass the purée through a sieve/strainer to remove any fibre or lumps. Taste and sweeten to taste if necessary with a little sugar syrup before using. It will depend on the ripeness of the peaches used.

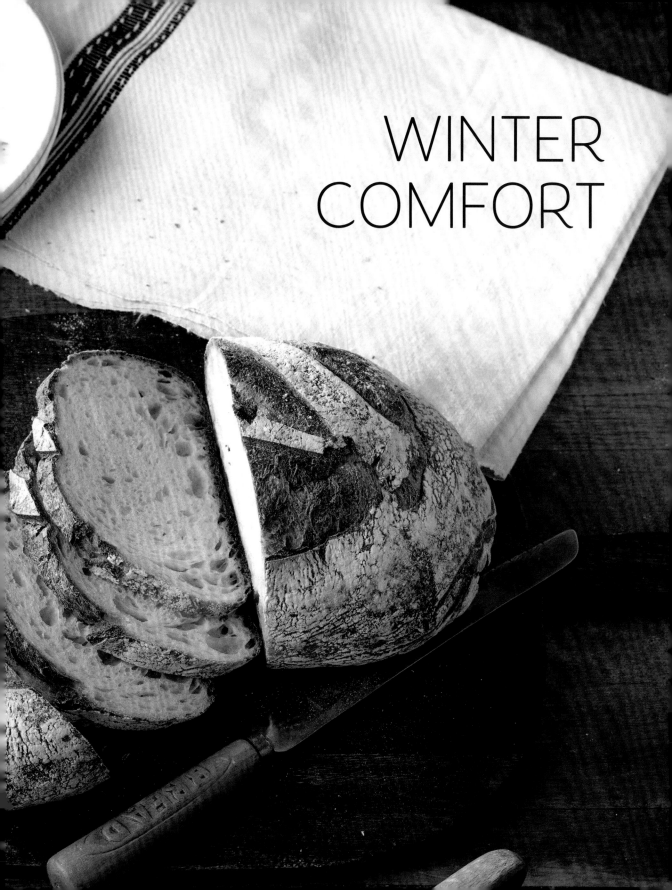

WINTER
COMFORT

STRAPATSADA

GREEK STRAPATSADA IS A THREE-INGREDIENT RECIPE OF SCRAMBLED EGGS WITH TOMATOES AND FETA CHEESE. THIS VERSION INCLUDES HERBS AND SPICES AND A LITTLE HEAT TO KICKSTART THE DAY, PLUS SOME CROÛTONS FOR A SATISFYING CRUNCH. IF YOU'RE FEELING CARNIVOROUS, ADD A FEW SLICES OF COOKED SMOKED SAUSAGE.

3 ripe tomatoes
2 tablespoons olive oil
½ green (bell) pepper, deseeded and sliced
3 spring onions/scallions, sliced
1 green jalapeño chilli/chile, sliced
½ garlic clove, crushed
¼ teaspoon ground cumin
¼ teaspoon paprika
½ tablespoon dried oregano
a pinch of sugar
80 g/3 oz. feta cheese, broken into large chunks
3 eggs, whisked
a handful of mixed green herbs, such as flat-leaf parsley, coriander/cilantro, dill and mint, roughly torn
¼ red onion, very thinly sliced
salt and freshly ground black pepper

CROÛTONS
1 slice of rustic bread, cut into 1.5-cm/½-inch cubes
2 tablespoons olive oil

SERVES 4

Preheat the oven to 220°C (425°F) Gas 7.

To make the croûtons, put the cubed bread in a bowl, season with salt and pepper and toss with the olive oil. Tip onto a baking sheet and bake in the preheated oven for 4 minutes, until golden and crisp. Remove and let cool.

Deseed the tomatoes and chop the flesh. Put the flesh in a sieve/strainer set over a bowl and let the juices run out.

Meanwhile, put the olive oil in a saucepan over a medium heat. Add the green (bell) pepper and spring onions/scallions and sauté for 2 minutes, then add the chilli/chile, garlic, cumin, paprika and oregano. After a further 2 minutes, add the drained tomatoes to the pan along with the sugar. Season with salt and pepper and simmer until the tomatoes have broken down, adding a splash of water if they start to dry out. When they are completely soft, turn down the heat and fold in half the feta cheese chunks and most of the fresh herbs, reserving some to garnish.

Using the back of a spoon, make a few indents in the tomato sauce around the edge of the pan and pour in the eggs. Now, still using the back of a spoon, drag a line from the eggs through the tomato mixture which will fill up with the runny egg. Do this several times, gently and slowly, until the egg is just about set, then remove the pan from the heat and let it rest for a few minutes.

To serve, gently slide the strapatsada onto a serving plate and scatter over the remaining feta cheese chunks, thinly sliced red onion, reserved herbs and the croûtons.

Serve with *Vodka Pickle Shot,* recipe on page 156

ROAST SQUASH & LENTIL SALAD

THIS IS SIMPLE TO MAKE AND SUCH A SATISFYING DISH TO EAT ON COLDER DAYS. THE SWEET BUTTERNUT SQUASH CONTRASTS NICELY WITH THE DARK AND EARTHY LENTILS, BOTH IN FLAVOUR AND APPEARANCE. IF YOU'VE GOT SOME FETA LURKING IN THE FRIDGE, THROW A FEW CRUMBS ON TOP TO SERVE.

1 x 1-kg/2 lb. 4-oz. winter squash, such as butternut, pumpkin, hubbard or acorn
about 4 tablespoons olive oil
a couple of pinches of dried oregano
a few sprigs of fresh rosemary
6 garlic cloves, unpeeled and halved
1 x 250-g/9-oz. packet of cooked Puy lentils
1 x 250-g/9-oz. packet of cooked green lentils
½ red onion, thinly sliced
100 g/3½ oz. cooked beetroot/beet, cut into wedges
a small handful freshly chopped flat-leaf parsley
about 2 tablespoons red wine vinegar, to taste
salt and freshly ground black pepper

SERVES 8 TO SHARE, 4 AS A MAIN

Preheat the oven to 200°C (400°F) Gas 6.

Peel and deseed the squash and cut the flesh into 2.5-cm/1-in. slices (if you are using butternut, you can leave the skin on as it will cook okay). Put the squash pieces in a bowl and add a glug of olive oil, the oregano, rosemary and garlic, then mix well.

Tip into a roasting pan and roast in the preheated oven for about 30 minutes, or until the squash is tender and cooked and starting to brown at the edges.

Tip both the Puy and green lentils into a large bowl and add the red onion, beetroot/beet wedges and chopped parsley. Dress the salad with a generous amount of the remaining olive oil and a splash of red wine vinegar – taste and adjust the balance of olive oil and vinegar to taste. Season with salt and pepper.

To serve, add the roasted squash to the bowl and fold it into the lentils, along with any cooking juices in the pan.

SMOKED HADDOCK ON SOURDOUGH

IF ANYTHING EPITOMIZES AN INDULGENT BRUNCH, IT'S GOT TO BE A COMBINATION OF FLAKED SMOKED HADDOCK, TOPPED WITH A POACHED EGG AND A BLANKET OF SLIGHTLY SHARP YET CREAMY SAUCE. HERE, THE POACHING MILK FROM THE FISH IS USED TO CREATE A LIGHT BUT NO LESS DELICIOUS FAUX HOLLANDAISE.

400 g/14 oz. smoked, undyed haddock

about 500 ml/2 cups full-fat/whole milk

1 dried bay leaf

4 slices of sourdough bread

a generous pinch of chilli/hot red pepper flakes (optional)

12 spears fresh asparagus

1 tablespoon butter

1 tablespoon plain/all-purpose flour

½ teaspoon English/hot mustard

½ teaspoon cider vinegar

4 eggs, or 12 quail's eggs, as preferred

freshly chopped flat-leaf parsley, to garnish

salt and freshly ground black pepper

olive oil, for brushing

SERVES 4

Put the haddock in a snug-fitting saucepan and pour in enough milk to cover. Add a few grinds of black pepper and the bay leaf. Poach on a low simmer for about 5 minutes, until the flesh is opaque. Leave the fish in the milk until cool before removing it. Set aside and reserve the poaching milk.

Brush the sourdough bread with olive oil, season and sprinkle with a pinch of chilli/hot red pepper flakes (if liked). Lightly oil the asparagus. Heat a griddle/grill pan until really hot. Add the bread and toast for 2 minutes on each side, warming the asparagus in the pan at the same time until lightly browned and nutty.

Set a small saucepan over a low heat. Add the butter and flour and heat for 2 minutes or so to cook out the flour, then whisk in 125 ml/½ cup of the reserved poaching milk. Bring to a simmer, continuously whisking until you have a smooth, creamy sauce,

adding more milk to achieve your desired consistency. Add the mustard and vinegar, stir, taste for seasoning, and set to one side until needed.

To poach the eggs, bring a small saucepan of water to a simmer, swirl the water then slide an egg out of its shell and into the centre, poach for about 5 minutes until the white is cooked, then carefully remove with a slotted spoon and drain on paper towels (if using quail's eggs, only for 1–2 minutes). You may need to poach the eggs in batches.

Place the toasted sourdough slices on a serving board with the flaked fish and asparagus arranged on top, add the soft poached eggs and pour over as much faux hollandaise sauce as you fancy. Sprinkle some freshly chopped parsley over the top to garnish and add a grinding or two of black pepper.

Serve with Homemade Gingerade, *recipe on page 154*

TURMERIC PANCAKES WITH CARROT HUMMUS & SHREDDED VEGETABLES

PANCAKES ARE ALWAYS A WELCOME ADDITION TO THE BRUNCH TABLE, AND THESE ONES HAVE A SAVOURY FLAVOUR AND VIVID COLOUR DUE TO THE TURMERIC IN THE BATTER. YOU CAN VARY THE FILLING BY USING WHATEVER VEGGIES ARE IN SEASON.

2 teaspoons cumin seeds
150 g/1¼ cups chickpea/gram flour
2 teaspoons ground turmeric
½ teaspoon salt
1 tablespoon olive oil, plus extra for frying

CARROT HUMMUS
500 g/1 lb. 2 oz. carrots, peeled and roughly chopped
1 tablespoon olive oil
1 x 200-g/7-oz. can chickpeas
1 small garlic clove, crushed
freshly squeezed juice of ½ lemon
3 tablespoons extra virgin olive oil
¼ teaspoon ground cumin
salt and freshly ground black pepper

TO SERVE
1 cucumber, deseeded
1 large courgette/zucchini
1 bunch of radishes
150 g/5½ oz. podded peas
freshly squeezed juice of ½ lemon
1 tablespoon extra virgin olive oil
100 g/3½ oz. salad leaves
a handful of coriander/cilantro
extra oil, lemon juice and salt and pepper

MAKES 8 PANCAKES

Preheat the oven to 180°C (350°F) Gas 4 and line a roasting pan with baking parchment.

To make the carrot hummus, place the carrots, olive oil, salt, pepper and 1 tablespoon of water into the prepared pan and roast in the preheated oven, covered with foil, for 40 minutes until tender. Set aside to cool. Drain the chickpeas, reserving 3 tablespoons of their liquid. Purée the carrots, chickpeas and reserved liquid, garlic, lemon juice, extra virgin olive oil, the cumin and some salt and pepper in a food processor until smooth. Set the hummus aside.

To make the pancakes, toast the cumin seeds in a dry frying pan/skillet until golden; let cool. Sift the chickpea/gram flour, turmeric and salt into a bowl and stir in the cumin seeds. Make a well in the centre and beat in 350 ml/1½ cups cold water and oil to make a thin pouring batter. Rest for 15 minutes.

Meanwhile, thinly shred or slice the cucumber and courgette/zucchini. Halve or quarter the radishes. Blanch the peas in lightly salted boiling water for 2 minutes, drain, then refresh under cold water and pat dry. Combine the vegetables in a bowl and toss with the lemon juice, olive oil and some salt and pepper. Set aside.

Heat a frying pan/skillet over a medium heat. Drizzle with a little oil and then mop up with a paper towel. Pour in about 60 ml/¼ cup of the pancake mixture, swirling the pan to lightly coat the base. Cook over a medium-low heat for about 1½ minutes until the bottom is golden. Flip the pancake over and cook for a further 30–60 seconds until dotted with brown. Transfer to a low oven to keep warm. Repeat to make 8 pancakes.

To serve, spread a little carrot hummus onto each pancake, scatter over the shredded vegetables, salad leaves and herbs. Wrap, roll, flip and serve drizzled with a little extra oil, lemon juice and black pepper.

POPPY SEED PANCAKES WITH CRUSHED CINNAMON RASPBERRIES

THE BEST METHOD WITH THESE FANCY PANCAKES IS TO POUR IN THE BATTER AND ONCE THE TOP IS ALMOST SET, ADD THE RASPBERRY MIXTURE, THEN SPOON OVER MORE BATTER AND CAREFULLY SPREAD THIS OVER THE FILLING. ALLOW A FEW SECONDS BEFORE FLIPPING OVER TO COOK THE SECOND SIDE OF EACH.

60 g/scant ½ cup self-raising/
  rising flour
1 teaspoon baking powder
2 eggs, separated
50 ml/3½ tablespoons buttermilk
1 tablespoon melted butter
¼ teaspoon vanilla extract
2 teaspoons poppy seeds
25 g/2 tablespoons caster/
  granulated sugar
vegetable oil, for frying
icing/confectioners' sugar,
  to serve

RASPBERRY FILLING
100 g/scant 1 cup fresh
  raspberries, plus extra to serve
1 tablespoon caster/granulated
  sugar
¼ teaspoon ground cinnamon

MAKES 8

Begin by making the raspberry filling. Place the raspberries, sugar and cinnamon in a bowl and mash with a fork. Leave to marinate for 10 minutes, then strain and discard the juices. Set the crushed cinnamon raspberries aside.

Meanwhile, to make the pancakes, sift together the flour and baking powder. In a bowl, beat the egg yolks, buttermilk, butter and vanilla and then whisk in the flour and baking powder. Fold in the poppy seeds.

In a separate bowl using a hand-held electric whisk, beat the egg whites and sugar together for 2–3 minutes until stiff peaks form. Stir a third of the mixture through the batter and then carefully fold in the rest until evenly combined.

Heat a frying pan/skillet over a low heat and brush with vegetable oil. Pour about 30 ml/2 tablespoons of the batter into the pan (two portions at a time) and cook over a medium-low heat for 1 minute. Carefully spread 2 teaspoons of the crushed raspberry mixture in the centre of each pancake and as soon as the edges of the pancakes are starting to set, spoon over enough of the batter to coat the filling.

Continue cooking the pancakes for a further 1 minute until almost set, then flip over and cook for a further 30 seconds or until golden underneath and set. Remove the pancakes from the pan and keep them warm while you cook the remaining batter in the same way.

Dust the pancakes with icing/confectioners' sugar and serve with a few fresh raspberries.

Serve with a *Pear Bellini,* recipe on page 43

Homemade Gingerade

*Stave off the winter blues with an easy to make
gingerade that's oh so refreshing but warming too.*

200 g/1 cup demerara/ turbinado
  sugar
40 g/4 tablespoons peeled and
  grated fresh ginger
freshly squeezed juice of
  6–8 limes
200 ml/¾ vodka or gin (optional)
a bunch of mint leaves, gently
  bruised
ice cubes
club soda or sparkling water,
  to top up
lime slices, to serve

SERVES 6

Place the sugar, grated ginger and 250 ml/1 cup of water in a saucepan
or pot set over a medium heat. Stir continuously until the sugar has
dissolved. Bring to the boil, then immediately reduce the heat and
simmer gently for 10 minutes. Remove the pan from the heat and set
aside to cool for at least 1 hour (the longer it infuses, the more gingery
your syrup). Add the vodka or gin once cool, if using.

Add the lime juice and bruised mint leaves. Half-fill your serving jug/
pitcher or highball glasses with ice. Pour in the ginger-lime syrup (about
60 ml/¼ cup per person). Top up with soda water/club soda, add lime
slices and serve.

Pictured on page 155.

Blood Orange & Rosemary Negronis

*When blood oranges are in season make the most of them in this Negroni.
If you prefer to use normal oranges, they also work really well. This is not
sweet but has a clean and light sour taste, a flavour that is great
with savoury dishes.*

150 ml/⅔ cup Campari
150 ml/⅔ cup sweet (rosso)
  vermouth
100 ml/scant ½ cup gin
3–4 blood oranges, cut into
  wedges
8 sprigs of rosemary
ice cubes

SERVES 6–8

Half-fill a large jug/pitcher with
ice cubes. Add the Campari,
vermouth and gin and stir to
combine. Refrigerate until
ready to serve. Add more ice
and garnish with blood orange
wedges and rosemary sprigs just
before serving.

Pictured opposite.

Fireside Sangria

Who said rosé wine was just for summer? Here is a sparkling brunch punch to cosy up with on colder days. It makes a refreshing and welcome alternative to the ubiquitous mulled wine at any festive gathering.

about 10 seedless white grapes, halved lengthways
about 10 seedless red grapes, halved lengthways
1 small orange, finely sliced
90 ml/3 oz. Grand Marnier, or other orange-flavoured liqueur
90 ml/3 oz. sweet red vermouth
170 ml/¾ cup clementine juice or blood orange juice
375 ml/1½ cups fresh, fruity Sauvignon Blanc
1 x 750-ml/25-oz. bottle of rosé Prosecco, well chilled
dried orange slices and cinnamon sticks, to garnish
ice cubes

SERVES 6–8

Put the grapes and orange slices in a punch bowl. Pour in all the other ingredients, including plenty of ice cubes and stir.

Serve ladled into ice-filled tumblers or red wine glasses and garnish each one with a dried orange slice and a cinnamon stick.

Pictured opposite.

Vodka Pickle Shot

This warming vodka pickle shot can be made with just four ingredients. Batch, bottle and chill to serve a group.

30 ml/1 oz. vodka
30 ml/1 oz. pickle juice/brine
¼ teaspoon celery salt
¼ teaspoon chilli/chili powder
ice cubes

SERVES 1

Stir together the celery salt and chilli/chili powder in a small bowl. Pour out onto small plate. Dip the rim of a shot glass into some pickle juice and then dip the wet rim into the spice mixture.

Fill a cocktail shaker with ice. Pour in the pickle juice and vodka. Shake for a few seconds and then pour into your prepared shot glass. Serve immediately.

Pictured on page 144.

INDEX

RECIPE CREDITS

VAL AIKMAN-SMITH
Apricot & basil mimosas
Mango pepper boba
Mojitos with lime sea salt
Summer sangria

JULIA CHARLES
Fireside sangria
Just peachy punch
Rosé, bourbon & blue
The pink & the green
Vodka pickle shot

LIZ FRANKLIN
Aperol spritz
Classic negroni
Classic white peach Bellini
Fig, blue cheese & rocket
pizzette
Fresh spinach & herb frittate
Pear bellini
Strawberry & basil bellini
Tinteretto

LAURA GLADWIN
Jasmin blossom
Mimosa

TORI HASCHKA
Beergarita granita

CAROL HILKER
Caprese skillet
Chicago strata
Chorizo nacho skillet with
homemade tortilla chips

Fisherman's wharf benedict on
sourdough
Fried 'baloney' sandwich with
dill mayo & fries
Maple-cured bacon & tomato
sandwich
New Orleans Benedict
Oyster Rockerfeller hash
Paris-style eggs benedict
Pretzel croissants
Steak & egg breakfast tacos

VICKY JONES
Korean moong pancakes
with pork

KATHY KORDALIS
Blood orange & rosemary
negronis
Cool & dirty martini
Elderflower sparkle
Flavoured waters
Green piña colada smoothie
Kir Royale
Lime martini
Lime, cucumber & lychee gin &
tonic
Margaritas with jalapeños
Pancetta & egg tart with
tomato chutney Pomegranate
& mint green tea
Pomini
Rose martini
Rosé spritzer with rose tea
buds
Salade de chevre with edible
flowers
Watermelon fizzy punch
Whiskey iced tea

UYEN LUU
Banana fritters

THEO MICHAELS
Blueberry, coconut & chia seed
mini açai bowls
Churros with mocha dip
Citrus salad with rosewater
caramel
Fennel & green apple salad
Mediterranean rosti with green
tomato sofrito
Ouzo-cured salmon bagels
Ricotta pancakes with cherry
compote
Roast squash & lentil salad
Rosé-roasted rhubarb &
pistachio yogurt pots
Smoked haddock on sourdough
Smoky aubergine shakshuka
Socca with charred asparagus
& labneh
Strapatsada
Spanish-style tortilla with
fresh tomato salsa

HANNAH MILES
Buttermilk pancakes with
salmon & horseradish cream
French toast with asparagus &
hollandaise

LOUISE PICKFORD
Baked egg pancakes with
tomato relish, chorizo &
avocado
Beetroot pancakes with goat's
cheese, onion relish & walnuts
Cauliflower & chickpea pacos
with tahini & lime yogurt

Poppyseed pancakes with
crushed cinnamon raspberries
Seeded baked pancake with
berries & cocoa sauce
Turmeric pancakes with carrot
hummus & vegetables

SHELAGH RYAN
Spicy pork burgers with mango
salsa
Best-ever Bloody Mary
Butternut squash with eggs,
cavalo nero, feta & jalapeño
zhoug
Caponata with grilled polenta
& whipped feta
Coconut chia pudding pots
with mango & mint
Fish finger baps with cucumber
& radish pickles
Hibiscus iced tea
Homemade gingerade
Pancakes with banana, salted
caramel & toasted pecans
Smashed avocado on toast
with courgette & herb salad
& dukkah
Strawberry, banana & almond
smoothie bowl
Superfood bowl with smoked
salmon, quinoa & avocado

PICTURE CREDITS

KATE WHITAKER
Photographer and prop stylist

ANNIE RIGG
Food stylist
Pages 1, 2, 4–5, 9, 10–11, 17, 18,
21, 27, 28–29, 33, 35, 36, 44–45,
49, 53, 55, 60–61, 62, 63, 65,
76–77, 81, 83, 92–93, 97, 103,
110–111, 115, 116 (inset), 117,
124–125, 129, 133, 142–143, 148
(inset), 149 & 153.

MOWIE KAY
Pages 3, 24, 25, 30, 39, 56, 71, 72,
75, 79, 87, 88, 89, 91, 107, 120,
126, 131, 135, 136, 139, 144, 147
& 155.

ALEX LUCK
Pages 6, 40–41, 42, 59, 108, 121,
141 & 157.

ADRIAN LAWRENCE
Pages 12, 98, 104 & 112.

IAN WALLACE
Pages 22, 66, 84 & 150.

TOBY SCOTT
Pages 15, 94 & 101.

PETER CASSIDY
Pages 46 & 67.

CLARE WINFIELD
Page 119 & 122.

STEVE PAINTER
Page 50.

ISOBEL WIELD
Page 73.